AF699983

Sept 18, ...

To Kenny,

Thank you for all your help.

Put one egg in real estate!

Hilda

Real Estate 101 Buying
Real Estate 102 Renting

All You Need To Know To Invest In Real Estate Successfully

HILDA'S BASICS

LEARN HILDA'S WAY OF MAKING YOUR INVESTMENT A SUCCESS

by

HILDA GIRON ERFE

CLIFF WALK PRESS

Lincoln, RI

Cliff Walk Press
P.O. Box 339
Lincoln, RI 02865.
www.hildashouses.com

Disclaimer

This publication is designed to provide accurate and authoritative information in regard to the subject matter covered. It is sold with the understanding that the author and publisher are not engaged in rendering financial, legal, accounting and other professional services. If expert assistance is required, the services of a professional should be sought.

The author and publisher specifically disclaim any liability or loss that is incurred as a consequence of the use and application, directly or indirectly, of any information presented in this book.

LIBRARY OF CONGRESS CATALOGING-IN-PUBLICATION DATA

Erfe, Hilda Giron.
Real estate 101 buying, real estate 102 renting:
all you need to know to invest in real estate successfully:
Hilda's basics / Hilda Giron Erfe.
p. cm.
"Learn Hilda's way of making your investment a success."
LCCN 2002095099
ISBN 0972503242

1. Real estate investment. 2. Rental housing. I. Title.

HD1382.5.E74 2003 332.63'24
QBI02-200808

This book is dedicated

to my husband, Albert, who always says NO!

to my son, Vincent, who can use my experiences to his benefit.

and

to my father Francisco V. Giron, (deceased)
and my mother, Artemia M. Giron,
for unknowingly giving me their best genes.

Acknowledgements

For the resourcefulness of Lynn LaFontaine of Trident Mortgage, for searching for the best mortgage rates, and for her speed in the closing, which is important in this kind of business.

I would like to thank my literary agent, Warwick Associates, for the patience they showed me during the course of the preparation of the book. Simon Warwick-Smith has had good foresight about the book. He called me right away as soon as the first draft came in.

To Patty Vadinsky of Warwick Associates, I give my grateful thank you. This book would not have been written if it were not for her explanation of what it takes to be a writer. I felt as though she was with me when I was doing the job in Newport as I related my experiences.

To the super team of Patty Vadinsky, Michele Filshie, Jim Hunt (our illustrator), Kathy Fulton (our book designer), and Karen Misuraca (our editor), I give my heartfelt thank you. Barbara Lewalski, Joan Clout-Kruse and Walter Semkiw for the time they gave me and their thoughts and advice. Also, thank you to my review readers for spending the time to dissect the manuscript. I enjoyed working with you all!

Helder Medeiros and Brian Frenette, my accountants, for surviving all of the surprises that I gave them. John "Jack" McGreen, my lawyer from Taft and McSally Law firm, for helping me go through the ups and downs of the problems involved in buying and especially renting the houses. For Eugene Simone and Marilyn Carroll of Merrill Lynch, I give a huge appreciation and thank you for taking care of my needs for over twenty-five years.

An unending thank you to Helder Medeiros for convincing Douglas Henson of First Federal Savings Bank of America to give me one of the LLC's capital home improvement loans.

I would also like to thank Marguerite Vadnais of Central Falls Credit Union for always attending to my mortgage needs immediately.

Patsy Ewenson, of Newport Rental Guide, my friend forever, for taking care of the houses when I go on vacation. Ed Coleman, for his thoughtfulness about first asking me when I will go on vacation before he makes his vacation plans. He makes sure that somebody is in the home front when I am away.

For all my business associates and tenants, who responded to my request for contributing their thoughts and enjoyment in working with me and for staying at my houses. You are the best!

To LTJG Jason Schwarzkopf, USNA '97 and US Navy, for being my good luck, "Buena Mano."

TABLE OF CONTENTS

Real Estate 101 Buying
Real Estate 102 Renting

CHAPTER 1 About the Author

While I was growing up in the Philippines, I saw my mother and father buying residential lots in Manila and a neighboring town, Tagaytay City, which is a resort town. Tagaytay City is on a ridge where you can view Taal Volcano surrounded by Taal Lake.

Mom and Dad

Whenever my parents bought a piece of land, they always paid installments for five years. They are business people and their surplus of money went towards buying real estate. They did not put money in the stock market, because it was not tangible to them in comparison to real estate. They started by purchasing small properties. My mother is the gutsy one and very good in business. She buys things and then tells my father later. My father was very mechanical. He completed two years of civil engineering school, and he could build anything. He has built an ice plant, a rice mill, and a coffee roaster He repaired trucks and his knowledge rivaled any graduate of civil engineering. He was also very resourceful when it comes to financing. He always went to different banks and lending companies searching for the lowest rate. My parents were a perfect match. While one was an expert in building machinery and repairs, the other handled running the businesses. My brothers and sisters and I were put to work as soon as we could wax the hardwood floor!

In 1950, my mother negotiated to buy an ice plant while my father was out of town. She consulted with their accountant, inquiring if the ice plant was for sale, and the price. My mother had 10% for a down payment in cash. She intended to ask my father if he could borrow 40% from elderly relatives. She would pay them back in six months. The accountant got the price, and my mother said, "Tell the owner that I will not counter offer. I will pay the asking price and give 50% as a down payment. I will pay back the remainder in three years." The deal went through. When my father came home from Manila, she told him the news. My father fell on the floor saying " Why did you buy that? I do not know anything about an ice plant." My mother responded. "Just buy two books and you will be alright." The life expectancy of an ice plant is about thirty years. The one that my father built lasted fifty years. My mother had to build a new one in the year 2000.

I must have gotten their good genes. I enjoy working and cannot be idle. I am always searching for something to do. I like dealing with people and I have a vast knowledge of different types of machinery, a quality that comes in handy, as a landlord.

Education and Experience

In high school, I taught catechism; in graduate school, I was a teaching assistant in the organic laboratory at Vassar College in Poughkeepsie, New York where I received an MS in Chemistry in 1966. I had a roommate at Vassar, Charlotte Yu, who was from Hong Kong. She taught me the basics of Chinese cooking. I owned a food company in the Philippines, and I supervised over one hundred workers who did different jobs in the processing plant. I started this company from scratch. I received my MS in Nutrition and Food Science in 1968 from the Massachusetts Institute of Technology in Cambridge, Massachusetts. At the same time, I taught basic food science at the Philippine Women's University (BS in Chemistry.) I taught cooking classes at my house, a do-it- yourself Oriental cooking class that I have taught over one hundred students, both women and men. I have owned a restaurant, and have taught the wives of Chinese graduate students at Brown University how to cook. I always believe that basic courses are very important to succeed in any endeavor that you tackle.

Getting into Real Estate

I did not read any real estate books when I first started buying houses. I followed my instincts very methodically, and solved problems when they arose. I am very organized and have a system. Since I have written this book, I have checked many bookstores and I have not found any hands-on books on real estate using the method that I use. I have never had a business partner to help me or advise me. I have done it all single-handed, and so can you!

After I purchased my eighth and ninth houses, I had enough experience to teach others what I was doing. I wanted this book to be easy to read, so that people would not be afraid of their ventures. It is also humorous and fun, and has some unbelievable stories that could be in a soap opera! It will provide stress relief. You will learn how to deal with lawyers, accountants, and realtors and how to interact with your associates.

Personally, I choose both single-family houses as well as duplexes to invest in for the following reason: When it is time to sell, the lower the value of the house, the more buyers can afford it. The higher the value of the house the fewer buyers can purchase it.

I was forty-nine years old when I bought my first timeshare in South Carolina. It is never too late to start!

I recently had lunch with my neighbor of twenty years, Pat Murphy, in Newport, the first time I had been out to lunch in Newport for quite some time. I am usually too busy and drive right past the restaurants. I showed her some of our rental properties in town and she said, "Oh my gosh, this is what you have been doing, you are so busy!" She asked what else I was currently doing, and I told her I was writing a book on investing in real estate. The first thing she said was, "Course 101 Real Estate Buying, Course 102 Real Estate Renting." She is absolutely right on track!

Basic knowledge is your most important lesson. Once you have that, you can do anything. Once you start to research a more advanced undertaking, you will learn that knowledge is the key to success and learning is "non-stop!"

Training Myself

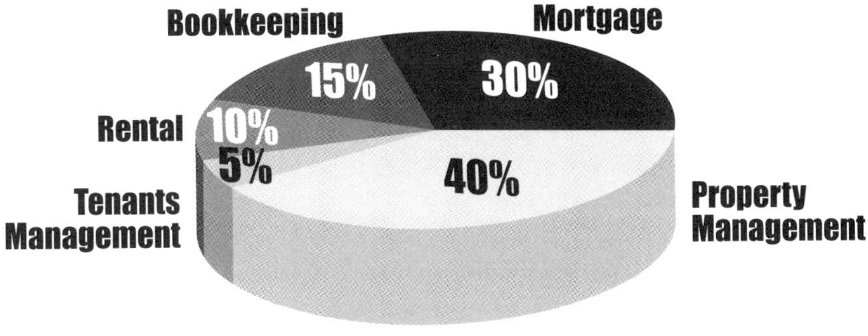

Focus

We should treat the world of real estate like a pie. A real estate agent can handle the rentals and the property management for you, but they are not responsible for paying the mortgages. I take responsibility for the whole pie, not just a piece of it. It is a hands-on job. I trained myself to focus, and I improve that focus as I continue to purchase more houses. I have to be very systematic. You cannot have the work take over your life, or cause you headaches. Managing rental houses should be enjoyable and should not make your life topsy-turvy!

Relax

Work during the day, and train yourself to relax at night. Jot down the things that you have to do the next day and you will rest easier. I usually have two or three scratch pads or post-it notes, each labeled with one of the next three days. For example on Sunday, I label one pad Monday, one pad Tuesday and one pad Wednesday. As soon as something pops into my mind, I write it down. If I am at an appointment or other commitment and I think of something I need to do within the next few days, I call my answering machine from my cellular phone and leave a message. Then when I get home, I write it on the appropriate note pad. You can also use a Palm Pilot, but I would probably misplace it. I also enjoy watching television, especially the business programs like Sue Herrerra on MSNBC in the afternoon.

Be Patient

Patience is another quality to develop. They say that you lose patience when you grow older. Well, you will need patience when dealing with finances and real estate. Your age does not matter. There are many service technicians, real estate agents, tenants and the like who will try to test your patience. Do not let them. After all these years, my patience becomes stronger each day.

Be Firm

Firmness is one quality that I certainly possess. Women are usually familiar with this one. We all know how to say, "no" to our children! When you believe the price is right, stick with your gut and don't budge!

Several realtors have asked me if I became frustrated and ever thought of giving up on a task or problem that I encountered. I simply answer, "It is part of the job, just do it. I always believe that if there is a problem, there is a solution."

Your Team

You will need a good team of reliable maintenance personnel. You will also need a good team of realtors who think of you first in terms of buying, renting, and eventually selling properties. Your accountant and attorney are also a part of the core to your success. When choosing my team, I requested that the candidates give me a short essay on their background, what services they could provide me and what products would assist me in carrying out the tasks of buying and renting houses.

As you can see from my background, I have had no formal real estate or financial training. I will relay my experiences, discuss what I have learned from my mistakes, and tell you how I went from putting a small down payment on my first house, to now managing over one million dollars in properties!

This book will give you all of the information you will need to know to invest in real estate successfully.

Here are my personal experiences, my methods and strategies. Follow my easy steps!

CHAPTER 2 Getting Started and Loans

In 1980, we were at a friend's house where our friend's son Norman Beretta showed us his new project in Newport, Rhode Island. It was an old bus garage that was going to be converted into fourteen condominiums. We did not have a second home, so we decided to buy one of these condominiums. It was in a great location within walking distance to the shops, restaurants, the park, the yacht club and the beach.

We used the Newport condominium for about three years, and then my husband grew tired of it. He was obsessed with keeping it neat and clean, and found it difficult to relax there. I looked at different possibilities of what we could do with this condominium. I rented it short-term. I did all of the cleaning when a tenant left. I do not like having year-round tenants at this property, because I want it kept in good condition at all times.

In the same year that we bought the condominium, my husband saw an advertisement in the New York Times showing a condominium for sale on Hilton Head Island in South Carolina. We thought this could be our winter retirement getaway. My husband went to Hilton Head while I stayed home with our young son. The unit he saw was furnished and still under construction with two bedrooms, two baths and a beautiful ocean view. The price for the unit was $89,000. We inspected it when it was ready. The first time we went on a vacation to our condominium, we did not realize that we had to reserve it. Our place had already been rented so we were given another unit, this one with bunk beds. My son just loved it! I never understood why my husband chose the back-end unit of the complex. I would have chosen oceanfront, which was only slightly higher in price at the time. Today, our resort is the only complex by the water that is in the $200,000-$250,000 price range. We made a terrific investment!

A few years later, my son left for college. I was forty-nine years old. I wondered what I would now do. I thought my life would be empty and void. After all, I had been devoting my time to driving my son around for thirteen years to school functions, activities, lacrosse and soccer games, etc, now I needed something to keep myself busy. I had a degree in Nutrition and Food Science. I tried working in food service at various jobs for about two years. For various reasons, I finally quit working in the food service industry. It was probably not right for me.

I was looking into buying a building in Providence, Rhode Island to open a restaurant. I think the price was about $250,000. I checked out the building, along with Norman, our friend's son, and felt it was worth only about $180,000. The owner was very insulted. I had applied to the bank for a mortgage, but never thought I would be able to borrow that sum of money. I forgot about opening my restaurant and backed out of the deal. After a few days, the bank manager telephoned me to ask if I was still buying the property. He told me I had been approved for the mortgage. I now had money along with the down payment I had already saved. I needed to buy something with it!

One day a real estate agent called to show me a house. This house had six bedrooms and was in a great location. I negotiated the price and bought the house. Closing the deal went smoothly, as I had already been pre-qualified for my mortgage. This was the start of my great adventure! I felt I had finally found my calling!

Loan Approval

Prior to looking for a house, it is wise to be sure that you qualify for a mortgage. A contract will be processed much quicker if you are pre-qualified for a loan. This will also give you an indication of the approved loan amount. You can begin this process by organizing your personal and financial information.

Start a separate file and label it Loan Information.

Order a copy of your credit report to check your credit history and to see if you have any outstanding balances. This usually costs under $100.00 and it can be ordered on the internet or over the telephone.

> **HILDA'S HINT**
>
> You can get your credit score online at www.myfico.com or www.equifax.com for a small fee.

Begin working on your balance sheet. You will be asked to prepare this as part of your loan paperwork. Gather all of your monthly credit card statements, car loans, existing mortgage or rent payments, and any other information, which shows that you receive income. Make copies for your folder.

Locate your IRS federal tax returns from the previous two years. If you cannot locate copies of your returns, they can be obtained through your accountant or the IRS. It may take a few weeks, not only to get through to the IRS by telephone, but also to receive your return! The loan process will be delayed by not having your tax returns readily available. Place these copies in your folder.

Obtain credible references from people who are not family. You may want to contact three or four business acquaintances or personal friends, making sure they are available should the lender need to contact them in checking your credibility.

Be ready…prepare for your loan interview. You should be well dressed, punctual, friendly and knowledgeable about your finances. If your spouse handles paying the bills and managing your bank accounts, discuss with them the basics for a better understanding of your finances. It is acceptable to ask questions of the lender, but you will need to be able to speak intelligently of your own financial capabilities. In my case, I am in charge of all the financial deals.

I remain qualified all the time. This makes closing a deal much easier. You must need to be prepared should a realtor call, or when the right house comes on the market. The last two houses I purchased, the buyers were not prepared to close on time. I had all of my information in hand and closed these deals! My records remain updated with my mortgage coordinator, and I inform her of any changes as they arise.

A Credit Story

I received a letter from a lending institution about my credit report, notifying me of a collection. Not understanding, I called Lynn LaFontaine from Trident Mortgage. She obtained my credit report and saw that I did not pay Verizon $53.65. All the bills that come to our primary residence were paid. I called Verizon and I talked to five customer service people and they all had different answers. They said I did not owe anything, so why the collection? Lynn always did my credit report and she researched the problem for me. She knows the ins and the outs on who to contact and how to find answers.

Every time a telephone, cable or utility bill is in my name, I specifically send the bill to my house. This Verizon bill was no exception. During the winter break, I always inspect the house's temperature. I noticed on one of the kitchen tables, some letters addressed to me. I saw Verizon's bill and called and apologized about the bill, and immediately sent in the payment. There was no collection notice from an agency. Lynn found the telephone number and the collection agency information. I called them and they said they did not put this error in the credit report. I called Verizon again and said the item was not put in to collection. I was as though Verizon threw a ball to the collection agency and it went back and forth until I got another customer service representative. This Verizon rep's name was Germano "Geff" Moreira. Verizon does not like to call the collection agency and vice-versa. Geff was the only one who could help me straighten out this situation. He said, "I was paid and there is no outstanding bill." I asked him to fax me a copy of proof that this was paid, and he did so within about five minutes. I brought the proof to Lynn and she called the collection agency immediately. They wanted the original bill, they did not want it faxed to them. I wanted the report corrected immediately. This Verizon 'bonanza' cost me 100 points down on my credit report. I paid the bills three months before this incident happened. Watch out!

HILDA'S HINT

Your credit history is the most important piece of information in the eyes of the lenders.

Bank or Mortgage Company

I previously used local banks for my mortgages. As soon as the interest rate was lowered, I would refinance to obtain a better rate. I searched everywhere to find the best mortgage rates. I read newspapers, magazines and watched television commercials. I advise that you keep a log of dates and interest rates, and pay attention to the trend. It may be possible that your local banks do not have the best rate.

HILDA'S HINT

Do your research! You will find a lower rate!

As interest rates dropped and I had a few houses to manage, I decided I would look for a mortgage coordinator. I was now in the business of buying and renting homes. I wanted to work with someone I could trust, and who would also look out for my best interest. I saw an advertisement in the newspaper for GMAC, contacted the company, and I was very impressed by the services and rates they offered. Now, I have seven mortgages with GMAC. Often times it takes a while to get accustomed to the different payments that must be sent to a mortgage company. I was assigned to a mortgage coordinator who now handles my needs. I transferred my accounts to this coordinator when she left GMAC and opened her own business, Trident Mortgage. I was very happy with her knowledge and service. She continues to take very good care of my needs. However, we still use GMAC as our mortgage company.

HILDA'S HINT

A mortgage coordinator will discuss with you the plans that best suit your needs and your budget.

I believe that a bank is more selective than a credit union. I have had dealings with Central Falls Credit Union. For an equity loan on a house, the bank offered me $35,000 while the credit union offered me $78,000. In comparison with the bank, the credit union took more time to analyze the information that I had submitted. My neighbor, Joseph Raheb, a lawyer, recommended Central Falls Credit Union to me.

There are also many advantages and benefits in working with a brokerage company. The brokerage company will also help you with your bookkeeping when you are traveling or if you need special assistance. Special arrangements can always be made; you just need to inquire of your account executive.

Down Payment

A. Saving

How did I go about saving for my down payment? I started saving money from the time my son was born, depositing it into a separate bank account. By the time he was ready for college, the tuition was so high that most of our expenses were spent on him! We are not an extravagant family, although we do like to eat out occasionally, and we enjoy a vacation in the summer. I saved a little money from each paycheck, and had no idea what I would do with this sum of money in my later years. I even saved enough to give my son a down payment on his first condominium!

There are many different types of loans on the market today. If you have never purchased a house before, you can still qualify to get a mortgage with a small down payment. Most of the companies will require a 20% down payment, but there are also some loans, with stricter guidelines, in which you can put 5-10% down, but you will need to purchase Private Mortgage Insurance, a subject covered later in the book.

The down payment depends on the lender or investor's specific guidelines. Remember that the mortgage company is the lynch pin for closing the deal. Without a mortgage, you will not have a house! There is one exception. It is possible that a property purchase can be made through your pension plan. Contact a financial advisor for more information regarding this option.

HILDA'S HINT

Prepare for your down payment ahead of time, so you will be ready to close the deal quickly!

B. Line of Credit

Another way to secure a down payment is to establish a line of credit from a bank. The interest rates are usually very competitive, and the amounts are standard, usually from $15,000 to $50,000. If you secure a $50,000 credit line, that does not mean that you have to use all of the money, you can use a portion of it. You spend as much as you need and then pay it down regularly. A line of credit usually has a variable interest rate, which your bank will review each year. There is also a fee deducted from your account, annually.

Refinancing & Equity Line

If you own the home where you live, you may be able to refinance. Refinancing is taking out another mortgage based on the equity that is already in your home. I would suggest first utilizing every other possible resource to obtain a down payment. Refinancing your current house should be the last resort. With refinancing, you will want to take your time in finding the best rate and lender. Do not rush into it because you need a down payment for another house.

A brokerage firm or financial institution can research whatever you need for the houses. When my houses were placed in a limited liability corporation (LLC) because of tax purposes as well as my sanity, I went around to lenders to see if I could take out an equity loan. Everyone told me that I could not, because they will not give a loan on corporations. I did not know about this policy. I should have gotten an equity loan first, and then transferred it into the corporation.

If you have a good relationship with your account executive, he or she can look for programs that will best suit you. If the houses are treated as business investments, the account executive will find a program to give you an equity loan. The house will serve as collateral. I am going to get an equity loan for each house. This will also be convenient for my accountant, as we will act as guarantor on the loan.

I also thought of getting a home equity loan for the two duplexes that I own. The estimate for exterior painting or vinyl siding is over $15,000.00! It will be impossible to pay for it with the rent, except by installments.

We have all the accounts at a large brokerage firm because it is more convenient to obtain loans there. If we pay off the first mortgage, it will be easier to buy stocks, bonds, mutual funds or a money market for the rental money. This is my foresight. Nowadays, you can go to any company that offers the convenience of investing!

I have a lot of equity in the houses, and the mortgages are in the vicinity of 17% to 25% of the appraised value of the first five houses that I bought from 1994 through 1997. I contacted my account executive, and he contacted the mortgage department to start the ball rolling. I filled out all of the necessary forms and sent them in to be processed. This began in the summer of 2001. I have had contact with the mortgage coordinator, but around October he seemed to have disappeared off the face of the earth! I told my account executive and he began checking around for me. Of course, my application was in limbo. Two other women searched through all of the outstanding paperwork, and finally in December, a supervisor contacted me.

The supervisor told me that since I have a first mortgage, I can refinance the houses for over 8%, but he did not tell me the term of the loan or how many years for the payoff. This is not a good idea for me because our current rate is between 7% and 7.5% and we have five to ten years left on the houses.

I asked about a home equity loan, and he told me that they will only give them to big businesses. No wonder they are laying off people, they have forgotten about small businesses like me! The supervisor also mentioned that he could only give 60% of the approved value of the home.

I have dealt with these people for a very long time. When I wanted to refinance a mortgage, it took a very long time for them to get back to me, so I ended up going to another lender. My account executive intended to serve his client well, but he had no control over how the mortgage company acts. He was a little bit upset.

In the early 1990's, I obtained a home equity loan through this same account executive for our Hilton Head property. They gave me 80% of the appraised value. Over the last few years we had paid off the first mortgage from another company, and we kept the home equity loan from them only for tax purposes.

The supervisor of the mortgage department should have looked at our record. When we pay off a first mortgage, I usually keep only the equity loan and do not get another mortgage.

My accountant recommended a local bank to me for the equity line. He has a lot of dealings with them for some of his other clients. He convinced them to give the LLC a "fund capital improvements to investment property."

HILDA'S HINT

Remember you can also use your equity line for repairs on your house(s).

The Vice-President of the bank's business department handled all of the transactions. It took less than four weeks for completion. What a relief! I can now vinyl side or paint the two duplexes! I am looking for other lending institutions to give me a home equity loan on the other LLC's.

Reserve Money

To avoid worry, devise a way to reserve money. Here are a few suggestions of how to get started:

A. Apply for a credit line if you have a business.

B. Keep the credit cards that have a higher limit.

C. Continue to save. If you have conditioned yourself to save from the beginning, you will always save.

D. Take an equity loan from your existing house.

I would like to give you an example of why a reserve account is so important. Of my nine houses, I had four houses that were not rented for the winter season. I have never had a problem renting, because the real estate group will usually provide me with information on renters during the summer. I realized this problem about two months before the winter season would begin in Rhode Island. I noticed that the rental agents that usually handled my houses had been assigned to different jobs in their company's office. This is a true test of how good my relationship is with the agents in Newport. By the first week of September, I had many other calls from other agents for monthly rentals. In turn, I asked them to show me some of the houses they were listing for possible purchases. Since I had a reserve account set-up for each house, it would not have been too devastating to my personal accounts if the houses were not rented for a month or two. I would have been able to cover the mortgage and any necessary repairs with the money in my reserve account. This also taught me a lesson—I changed my strategy of renting for the coming year.

HILDA'S HINT

If you have a reserve account, you can sleep easier knowing the bills will always be paid!

YOU CAN DO IT! $$ TEST AND GUTS

Again I will mention that it depends on the lender's guidelines, as to how much of a down payment you will need. In 1994, I had enough money for a 30% down payment for the first house. Following this first purchase, the subsequent houses were all lower in purchase prices. With lower down payments, I was able to buy more houses. By the time I was ready to buy my eight and ninth houses, I was only required to put 10% down, but I had to take the Private Mortgage Insurance or PMI. After I cosmetically fixed the appearance of the eighth house, the appraised value went up and the market value of the neighborhood was on the rise, so I was able to refinance after six months. My PMI was also eliminated.

I have guts…when I plan to do something *I JUST DO IT!*

CHAPTER 3 Buying a House

Now that you have completed your preliminary paperwork, and have been approved for financing, you are ready to go on a house hunting expedition! You will look to at many houses before you will find one that is right for you, and your budget. You will need to find a realtor that you can trust and who can help you to meet your requirements for the house. Realtors are usually very nice and eager, because they will make money whether you are buying or selling a house.

Working with a Real Estate Agent

There are many reasons why you should or should not work with a real estate agent. I have had both good and bad experiences, but I do consistently work with agents.

If you buy a house from an agent, they may help you find a renter. They will also contact you should a "good deal" arise that may be of interest to you.

There are various ways to find a real estate agent. Newspaper advertisements, open houses and walking into a real estate office are the most common. Ask your friends, business associates and local merchants whom they have used to buy or sell their home. A referral to a good realtor is most valuable. It is comforting to know that someone you trust has put his trust in another. The realtor likes to get referrals and he will tend to take more care with the referred client.

When you, in turn, refer someone else to that realtor they will most likely give you special treatment for your next purchase. They will also go 'the extra mile' to find renters for your house. Being loyal is very important in the real estate business, and it shows.

You will need to find a realtor and real estate agency that is considered to be "active." Along with the true meaning of the word, an active agent is one who fits the following criteria:

Familiar with the housing market in your area

Prepared to show you sales and houses they have rented in the past few months

Willing to work evenings and weekends

Works with an agency that is listing properties

Finding a good realtor will not always mean going to an agency whose name is nationally recognized or recommended. There are plenty of good local agents who are willing to help you find a house. You can call a few different agencies or walk in to check out the surroundings. Ask for the top selling agent or broker.

HILDA'S HINT

When in a real estate office look on the walls to identify the Million Dollar Club members, ask for one of those agents and tell the receptionist they are expecting you! You will most likely not be disappointed with this agent!

There are two types of real estate agents: a buyer's agent and a seller's agent. Most realtors are working for the seller, because they want to earn their commission from selling the property. On the other hand, the buyer's agent's sole fiduciary responsibility is to you, as the buyer. They will tell you everything they know about the property, whether it is good or bad, which can be to your advantage. They will also tell you if the seller's agent has indicated that the seller will take a lower price for the property.

Well, what is in it for my agent then, you ask? The buyer's agent's fee is usually half of the selling agent's commission. Many times a deal is worked out at the time of closing on the property, at which the seller agrees to pay both realtors commissions. This is particularly true if the house has been on the market for some time, and the sellers are getting anxious to sell! There is usually no extra out of pocket expense for the buyer, when using a buyer's agent.

You can make both yours and your agent's lives much easier, by having your agent give you a list of houses that they are planning to show to you. On your own time, drive by the house, inspect the neighborhood, and check the condition of the house and the yard. Then you can decide if you would like to pursue and view the inside and backyard. This will save you both time, and you can "weed out" the houses that you are not interested in for one reason or another.

It is also a good idea to check out open houses. Just be sure to remember if you like the house not to sign with the seller's realtor, if your realtor is not present. Your agent has invested time in you, and it is unethical not to include them in the sale.

In the early 1990's, I bought three houses from one real estate agency. They soon discovered that I was a "gold mine." They helped me find renters for my condo. One fall season, this agency completely ignored finding renters for my houses. They told me to ask other realtors to rent them for me, but it was too late. I wished had have known sooner.

Loyalty is very important to me. I would have rather stayed with this original realty company than to switch my business to another. This was an instance when I had to use my reserve money. I finally discovered that these realtors were told to rent their properties first before renting mine. I called all the local real estate agencies in Newport, and had an open house the next day for the realtors. This happened to be a blessing in disguise. I met many wonderful, friendly, well-mannered, pleasant, and reliable realtors. I have been doing business with most of them to date. I now always buy houses from the realtors who help me to rent my other houses. It is simply the principle of give and take.

HILDA'S HINT

Keep realtors who are loyal to you

For the purchase of one of my houses, a realtor required my husband to sign the sales agreement before I could make an offer to buy the house. When my husband is involved it is harder for me to negotiate. He usually says "no" to everything! In this instance he did sign the papers. Another realtor that I had met at the open house recognized the type of houses that I was interested in, and she called me and showed me a house, which I eventually purchased. I now had a new rule. I will buy a house on one condition, that my husband cannot get involved and he will just sign the papers at the closing. She said yes that would be fine, and the sale went through. The first realtor I had dealt with, found out about the sale after I had put it on my rental listing. She asked why I did not call her to negotiate the house. I told her that her company did not allow me to sign by myself. They learned their lesson, and so did I.

Spotting Value in a Property

A. Flow of Rooms

There is a certain feel to the flow of the rooms as you enter a house. If the house is divided, then you will easily see where the living room, dining area, kitchen, bathroom, bedrooms, and laundry room (in an older house, it is usually in the basement) are positioned. Look at where the doors are situated. Also take into account the hallways, and the floors.

Some owners have "chopped up" their houses, which destroys the flow of the rooms. How do you describe a "chopped up" house? I looked at one house where the owner had put a Jacuzzi in the family room, made a living room out of a small bedroom, turned a very small dressing closet into a bedroom; and a tiny hallway leading to the basement was turned into a half bathroom. With the rooms situated this way, the house will not work for 99% of the population. It will also be very difficult to resell.

Another thing to keep in mind: will you make money when you want to sell this house? My first home was a three-bedroom house. My husband and I both liked this house, but we did not think about the steep driveway. It was so steep that the snowplow refused to clear it. We purchased the home in the summer, and coming from a region where there is no snow, we were unaware of the trouble this would cause. We lived there for nineteen years and learned how to deal with the inconvenience because we liked the house. When we sold this house (within a week), the buyer did not mind the driveway and we tripled our money on the sale. The rooms flow proportionally, it has a beautiful view, and we had maintained it, and had put a lot of time, effort and money into the landscaping.

B. Location

Always check the location of the property. Remember that old cliché...location, location, location. Are the houses around it in good condition? Is it in a residential area? Is it near a shopping area? Is it near the most attractive center of town? If the area is a water resort, is the property waterfront, or in close proximity to the beach?

C. Records

Research the property. Start by going to City Hall where you can look up records of past sales and other information on the house. You should also check the original selling price and verify the age of the house. Compare this house to others in the area that have been sold, and to those that are currently on the market. This will insure you that you are not over paying.

D. Viewing the House

My favorite part of viewing a house is going into the basement. You can really see the soul and the backbone of the house. You will notice if the plumbing and electrical systems are up to date. The electrical system is usually 60 amps (for older houses). It will probably need to be updated to 100-150 amps, because of computers, several TV's, new technological gadgets, etc. If the electrical wires are old, then they will also need to be upgraded. If the plumbing has some PVC pipe, then the current homeowners have done some refurbishing.

HILDA'S HINT

Check the home's foundation. Look to see if there are any signs of water in the basement or any watermarks on the walls. If there are, most likely the foundation will need to be repaired. This can be a big headache! You may want to think twice about buying this house.

E. Bedrooms and Bathrooms

For a rental property it is wise to purchase a house with at least three or four bedrooms and a minimum of two bathrooms. The more bedrooms in the house, the more rent you can charge. I am now only buying houses with five or more bedrooms. I also only purchase houses with at least two bathrooms. Even if one is only a half bathroom, it will cause fewer headaches and fewer emergencies in the future. If there is only one bathroom in the house and the toilet breaks, your tenant will call you at all hours of the day or night because it is truly an emergency. If there are two bathrooms, they will not see the need to wake you up in the middle of the night because they will have another bathroom that can be used.

A one-bathroom house is also very difficult to resell. Even for a single person, a guest bathroom is still important.

HILDA'S HINT

Buying houses with four or five bedrooms and two bathrooms allows maximize rental rates when you have a large group of people like a sailing crew or regatta!

Condominiums and Townhouses

As mentioned earlier, I started in real estate with a two-bedroom condominium. The correct legal term for this type of property is attached housing. It is easier to get financing for condos and townhouses because of certain insurance criteria. A townhouse shares common sidewalls but there is no unit above or below yours. Paying monthly dues to a homeowner's association is almost always mandatory. The association normally handles the landscaping maintenance of all properties as well as exterior maintenance such as painting and roof repair. Each homeowner's association has by-laws that most states require you read and acknowledge prior to closing on the property.

There will always be something you will need to handle even with a condominium or townhouse. It is better for beginners to learn with a smaller property. With a condominium or townhouse you will also be dealing with parking, maintenance personnel, repairs, appliance breakdown, city hall regulations, plumbing repairs, furniture, cleaning and caring for the house, along with many other responsibilities. It is sometimes better to familiarize yourself on a smaller scale.

Buying Just before a Foreclosure

Sometimes you will run into a seller that is overly anxious to sell their house, and the word *time* is not in their vocabulary. I have run into two situations where sellers needed to close immediately so they could pay their mortgage and avoid bank foreclosure. In one situation, the husband told his wife that she had no choice but to sign the papers. When we were at the house closing, she tried to hold on to the property until the very last minute. She was very distraught because they had to sell their home. They were able to save their good credit rating.

I have not ventured into the area of bank foreclosure sales up to this point. It would be best to discuss this with your realtor and lender because there are different stipulations and rules that need to be followed with a foreclosure. Getting a good bargain on a house for little money is not always the best way to go.

Fixer-Uppers

I enjoy making cosmetic repairs and fixing electrical and plumbing systems, but it is certainly not for everyone. Buying a house to renovate takes a lot of time, knowledge, patience and most of all…money! Remember that you will most likely have to live in this house while you are working on it, unless you have another residence. Repairs and renovations are not as easy as they appear on television shows.

If you fix-up a low-end property for a rental, you will not always be able to charge enough rent to cover your expenses for the renovating. Before purchasing a house, which will need extensive repairs, prepare a worksheet with the pros and cons of attempting this project. List what obvious repairs will need to be made and the approximate costs. Remember to include painting, and new carpeting, as many older houses will need cosmetic work as well. Research how much the other rents are in the surrounding neighborhoods and see if it will be worth your while. It is rewarding to see the fruits of your labor once the work is complete, but if you will lose money in the long run it will certainly not be worth the effort!

Home Inspection

A home inspection is one of the most important elements in the purchase of a house. After initially viewing the house, I bring my team of professional maintenance personnel to the house for their inspections. Aside from the obvious flaws, perhaps the house needs a new roof or there is dry rot on the garage door. A home inspector will crawl through the attic, under the house and look in every nook and cranny to be sure this house has no hidden problems.

Your realtor will be able to recommend a home inspector. You can also look in the Yellow Pages, but if a home inspector is not recommended to you, I would suggest getting two or three references and calling those clients. After all, you do not want to find out months after purchasing the house that the foundation has a crack in it and your home inspector did not do a thorough inspection. Most sellers now expect a buyer to have a home inspection completed. There is usually a disclosure statement when you first view the house. The seller's agent will provide this information for you.

The seller's disclosure statement has little worthwhile information when you first look at the house. I now expect the seller to pay for the home inspection, and indicate this request when signing the sales and purchase agreement.

You should accompany the home inspector on the day of the actual inspection. Well, you do not have to crawl under the house, but you can certainly observe the inspector and he will explain potential problems or complications to you.

After deciding to purchase my ninth house, a duplex, I notified all of my business associates when the closing date was set. The business associates included the maintenance personnel, electrician, plumber, painter, and the gutter man. I told them that in six weeks the house needed to be in rentable condition. They agreed. I settled on a renter, and began work on the house. I expect each of my business associates to do their job each and every day, so we are sure the houses will be ready for the renters. I have dealt with these people for many years, and they each know what I expect.

The first floor was completed and ready for the first renter. The following week the second floor was finished and ready for the next group to move in. The work was done on time. This was the second house that my maintenance personnel and I fixed and everything went smoothly. If the work had not done on time, the town of Newport would have seen a mad and screaming woman running rampant on the streets! We are all glad that this did not happen!

Homebuyers are as unique as the homes they plan on buying. However, one thing all buyers do have in common is a desire to know as much as possible about their prospective investment. The house they are buying is probably the most expensive investment they will ever make.

Standard inspection components: exterior home components, electrical systems, roof, foundation- interior and exterior, heating/ air conditioning systems, plumbing systems, attic, basements/ crawl space, room by room…. and more.

Other services offered may include: radon gas testing, water analysis, mold testing, wood destroying insect inspections, septic testing, carbon monoxide testing, energy assessments, reserve studies, lead based paint testing, new home construction reviews, pool and spa inspections, commercial building inspections and much more.

When the inspection is done you receive a comprehensive written report detailing all the specifics of your home inspection.

Do not forget to ask about the rates!!!!

Final Inspection

On the day on or before your house closing, you should have a final walk through of the house with your realtor. It is a very good idea to indicate in your sales agreement that the sellers will move out at least twenty-four hours before the closing. This will give you the chance to see the house without the furniture or pictures on the walls etc. This will be the last time you will view the house before signing the final closing papers.

This is also the time to see if the previous homeowner has left any items that you had requested stay with the house in the sales agreement. Check the window treatments, carpeting, and appliances. If the seller has left any junk at the house, that they did not want to move, your realtor can contact the seller's realtor and have them remove it so you do not have to!

When I purchased my eighth house, I found that there were many items left at the house at the time of the final inspection. I withheld $500 from the closing in order to clean up this mess left by the seller. My attorney and my selling agent could not believe that I required this before I would sign the papers! They were very impressed with my follow-through and assertiveness.

Doing a Favor

I was nice once again. One of my maintenance people, who has worked with me for over six years approached me regarding a situation with his house. I got the impression that he had owned the house where he lived, but he now told me that he is renting the house and the owner informed him she is selling the house. This was an opportunity for him to take a shot on acquiring this house. However, he would not have a good credit report for about another twelve months. The asking price for the house was a bit high, as there was some work that needed to be done. I asked the seller to lower the price by $20K, and my offer was accepted.

The cooperation of the husband and wife played a big role in this sale. I tried very hard to overcome the obstacle that I was faced with, and I still could not see a bright light for this deal. My mortgage company coordinator helped my maintenance person figure out a budget for buying back the house from me within a period of twelve months. He could do it! I tried to back out of the purchase after realizing that there could be potential problems, but my mortgage coordinator told me that I would gain in the end, because the house appraisal came out $30,000 more than the asking price! So, I bought the house. The mortgage coordinator knew that I had purchased several fixer-upper houses, and that this deal would be no different.

The day after the house closing, I went over to the house and asked my maintenance man to give me a key so I could make a copy. I always keep a key to each one of my houses. He gave me a copy of his key and made a comment that disturbed me quite a bit. He said, "Now she wants the key! She will be here all the time and I will not have any privacy." I responded, "You know that I have keys for all of my houses for emergencies. I have a right to have a key…I own the house!" He told me in front of the realtor that I treat him "small." I was discussing the rent with him, and told him how much he owed. I told him that since I closed on the twenty-eighth of the month, he would have to give me the first month's rent. He had to pay rent to his previous landlord, so why should this be any different? He wanted to pay me the rent the twenty-eighth of the next month, which would mean that he would already be one month behind. I told myself that this was going to be a problem. He will not be able to pay. I know that he has a business on the side and that he makes good money, especially with the work he does with my properties. He informed me in front of the realtor that he will be leaving the house at the end of the month because I treat him "small."

I contacted my attorney and told him about this problem. He wrote my maintenance man a certified letter about his intended move. Everything was done the correct way. I am now fixing up the house and will try to resell. The maintenance person is not working for me anymore. I found out later he was having problems with his business.

HILDA'S HINT

Never get yourself involved in this kind of situation, especially with friends or employees. No matter how nice you are, and how much you are willing to help, you will be mistreated.

Because I buy rental properties, I need to make sure that the rent will be enough to cover the mortgage payment. You should still be aware that there might be some out-of-pocket expenses in order to pay the bills, especially in the case when you cannot rent because you are making repairs and upgrades to the house.

Negotiate

Now it is time to negotiate! Keep in mind that if you are buying for your residence, you need at least 20% down; if it is an investment, 30%, if you have several houses, 0 to 10% down. If the house is in good condition, I offer 10% less than the asking price. I will also go as far as 25% less than the asking price if the house needs a lot of repairs or sprucing up. If the house is overpriced, don't be afraid to lower your bid more, depending on the comparable prices of other houses in the area. You will go back and forth with the seller's realtor before arriving at the right selling price. Do not get discouraged. This is part of learning known as "the art of wheeling and dealing!"

HILDA'S HINT

Stick to your budget! Do not add anything that will cost more money. Remember that most repairs and expense will occur during the first five years that you own the house. You should only be doing major repairs when there is vacancy.

HILDA'S HINT

Do not budge from your price. Every increase in price means money out of your pocket.

Trend of Buying Property

I was asked to look at a property in April of 2002. The house was in a fairly good location, but not in the best area according to my standards. It needed some repairs and the asking price was $ 205,000. I offered the selling price and calculated that I would have to put in an additional $40,000-50,000 to get a decent rent for it, and a good return on my investment. That was on a Thursday and the realtor put a pending sale on the MLS. On Friday, I contacted my maintenance group to make an appointment to inspect the house on Monday and to get estimates on the work that needed to be done. All the paperwork was signed and mailed to the owner's mortgage company. I left a message on my realtor's voice mail telling her that we had to go to the house. On Sunday morning, while I was hosting my international group and we were shopping, I received a call from my realtor who told me that the owner of the realty company removed the pending sign on the MLS, in order to get some higher offers. The realtor asked me if I wanted to offer more money. I did not lose my cool when I heard this. I asked my realtor if she was involved with removing the pending sign. She said, "I would never do that to you." She knew what I would do if I discovered that she was involved. I would back out on all future deals. Trust is very important to me.

The offers went up to $245,000. Let us now talk about what commission the realty company got. Let us say that the commission is 4% (discounted), which would be $9800 divided to the buyer's and seller's agent, so that would be $4,900 for each one. The commission on a sale of the price that I offered of $205,000 would be $ 8,200. Therefore each realtor would get $4,100. My agent would now stand to get an extra $800 more from the higher priced deal. It is probably worth more to the owner of the realty company to get that extra $800, than to lose a buyer and seller like me. *Remember, I buy houses and one of these days I could sell.* This was a good lesson for me to learn.

HILDA'S HINT

If a realtor gets this greedy, it is good for the seller, but it is more than enough money out of the buyer's pocket. The buyer should not be a slave to his mortgage.

When a situation like this comes up, I usually do not step back two or three steps, but ten steps so I can look over the situation. My main concern is the mortgage. It would mean that I would have to pay a higher mortgage each month. What if I do not get enough rent to cover the mortgage? Then it must come from my reserve, and it would not be profitable for me.

Another incident happened following this one. I tried to negotiate to buy another property. One of the realtors in the same company presumed that I did not engage in a bidding war. I asked her what happened to my offer and she said, "The negotiation is a secret and you cannot participate in it." I think it is very disadvantageous to the seller if the listing agent refuses to inform another buyer of the bids. Her asking price was so high that the rent would not have been sufficient. However, I was approved by the bank for this higher asking price!

The sales and refinancing of the houses are at its height due to the more than thirty-year low in interest rates for real estate. The stock market softened also, so many investors have decided to put an egg in real estate. With the high selling price of houses, expect that the rent will hit the ceiling too. This is definitely the sign of a seller's market.

HILDA'S HINT

Save your cash! You will get a better deal when the real estate market softens.

When there are few available houses on the market to buy, the selling price of the houses will tend to be very high. It is not wise for an investor to give into a bidding war. Just hold on to what you have. This same trend happened in the early 1990's. I started buying houses in 1994, when foreclosures were in the newspaper daily. This was the start of the buyer's market.

CHAPTER 4 House Preparations and Personnel

You have purchased a house and are preparing for tenant screening and selection. Before having tenants walk through the house, be sure that all systems and appliances are in working order, and that the house is presentable for viewing.

HILDA'S HINT

Keeping up the appearance and condition of the house can be the difference between renting and not renting.

Since my houses are furnished, I have to deal with purchasing linens, furniture, pictures for the walls, all appliances and many other small details and tasks that unfurnished homes do not require. Some of my tenants, specifically the upper Naval officers prefer to have unfurnished houses, because they have their own furnishings and tend to live in the house between one and three years. I seldom rent the houses unfurnished, as it is difficult for me to move and store the dressers, beds and other furnishings.

All of my business associates should have a cellular phone, so that we can readily contact each other. I live one hour away from my rental houses, and I like to know that I can reach my maintenance team at a moment's notice. If they leave a message at my house, I will not retrieve it until late in the day. In the case of an emergency, that may be too late. We have to trouble-shoot immediately when there is a need for emergency repair. This is how you can measure if your maintenance personnel are qualified and good at their jobs.

We also send e-mails to each other to spell out the requirements and requests for jobs to be completed. I will usually have a meeting with my associates every now and then to update what has been completed and what work still needs to be done.

Finding and Keeping Reliable Personnel

I usually hire maintenance personnel through recommendations from realtors. Once I have hired one person, hiring others is like a chain reaction. When I needed a floor sander, the maintenance person knew one. Through recommendations from the sander, I hired a carpenter and a painter.

Honesty is the number one qualification I look for when hiring. Unfortunately you will probably not discover this until the person has been working for you for a while. If you see something unusual, observe and nip it in the bud before it is too late. I do not tolerate stealing. One time several tenants called me to inform me that some things were missing. A camera was taken, a new window that was to be installed in another house was gone, and even food from the refrigerator was eaten! I checked into the price of the camera. It was expensive, close to $300. I reimbursed the tenant for the camera, though it was not required of me, because tenants should have their own insurance to cover theft and damage. It is just part of good business. I had to fire one of the workers. We could not afford to have him in the group. I was no longer able to trust him to go inside the houses. After these incidents, there was no more theft.

I like to hire personnel with families and young children. I prefer if they have a full-time job and they work "on the side" for me to earn extra money. This helps the families with young children and many bills that go along with it. I also look for people who need extra money, when hiring employees. Especially at our production plant in the Philippines, I hire the wives of the men that my mother originally hired. The wives' earnings help to supplement the families income. They are reliable and trustworthy and are still working for us many years later.

When I bought my first rental house, the realtor recommended somebody she knew to handle the maintenance. In turn he recommended somebody to fix the pipes. After a week, the original maintenance person disappeared, and the second maintenance man (who fixed the pipes) was left. I discovered that he was in the Navy and he also maintained some other properties. He could do anything around the house. He cut the grass, sanded the floors, did some carpentry, and even got rid of some beehives. He could tackle any project that I threw his way. As I acquired more houses, it became too much work for him. The solution was to find some other help. He was also very good to the Navy tenants. He enjoyed reminiscing about the Navy life with them.

Another realtor recommended a few other personnel who I hired. One of the first jobs I had them do was to repair a broken toilet. After they fixed the toilet, the tenants called me the next day to say that it was still not working. I think that they just quickly fixed the chain and left. They had to go back several times to complete the repair, which meant several billings for me!

Another maintenance person was so fast in fixing and that he only stayed five or 10 minutes and then went to his next job. He was a disaster! He had fixed the caulking in the bathroom, and after a period of time everything began leaking in the ceiling. He also did not check for the stud in the wall when attempting to hang a picture or put up shelves. They always fell down.

It is very important for the maintenance person to focus when I give them an assignment. I will usually follow up to see if the work has been done. I will not usually say anything about it, but once or twice I may remind him of the job. I will also make sure that the job is written somewhere in their logbook. If the work is not accomplished in a timely manner, I will call someone else to do the repairs, and I do not inform the original maintenance person. This is one way to wake him up and have him move a little faster!

Some maintenance people take what I say regarding focusing on the job a bit lightly. This way it will stick in their minds. Instead of thinking through what I have said, others get insulted and they think that I am questioning their ability!

One time I went to a house to tell the tenants that we would be painting the two bathrooms while they were on their Christmas holiday. One of the girls told me that they had not used the second floor bathroom since September when they moved in. They said that the shower was broken. "I always repair things immediately," I told them. They said that they had told the maintenance person about the problem, but he never repaired it or told anyone else about it. I immediately called Roto-Rooter and scheduled an appointment for them to fix and change the hardware the following day. As soon as I got home, I changed all of the messages on my answering machines, to be sure that this will never happen again! Previously I had instructed my tenants to call my maintenance people directly. Now I instruct them to leave a message on my answering machine, to ensure I get every message.

I am very fair to my maintenance people.

HILDA'S HINT

Once or twice a year, I will usually ask my realtors the going rate for similar maintenance work in town. This enables me to stay updated on salaries for the maintenance personnel.

Outside Repairs:

Drive by your houses to assess what needs to be done for outside repairs. Prepare a schedule for who needs to complete what job. The tenants may not always notice problems on the exterior of the house. The roof, paint, landscaping, driveway, fence and porch need to be in tip-top shape at all times.

Inside Repairs:

The tenants are usually a big help in this area. After all, they want their living space to be comfortable and free of problems or hazards. When they move into the house, I have them list whatever they see that may need to be fixed. I do not have a prepared form; they can just give me a list so we can discover what we need to repair. Once they make their list, I drop by and give a copy to my maintenance person to look over and start going over the information they have given me. They begin the repairs immediately.

For example, if we have a leak on the ceiling, the plumber has to check the bathroom hardware and joints on the pipes. After that, we will be able to paint the ceiling. If the windows do not close properly, we will either fix or order new ones. I make a point of telling my tenants to report any faucet or toilet leaks. These must be repaired as soon as possible; otherwise the water bill can be greatly affected.

There are so many things to be done, I am very thankful that our tenants help us.

KEYS

There was only one key to the first condo I had purchased. Then came the second house that had three entrances, therefore there were 3 keys. As time went on and I acquired other houses, I now had many keys. I had inherited these keys from the previous owners, and there were so many of them that I have to devise a way to keep me sane! I was just starting out and I had very little money to spend on unnecessary items. We had locks or keys for each room, it was getting to be a disaster! The tenants would lose their keys or lock them inside of their bedroom. What put me over the edge with the key problem was getting a phone call while in New Jersey from a lady Navy officer who had locked her keys inside her room. To solve this problem we installed a sliding lock inside the room, so each tenant could have their privacy. After a year, I went to a local locksmith and inquired if they could re-key one of the houses. He came to the house and my life was now much easier. I am thrilled that I am no longer walking around with a purse load of keys. I am organized and can find any key to any door in any house at a moment's notice!

HILDA'S HINT

Look around until you find the best service technicians. When you find the right ones they will be your friends for life! They are my favorites, and I always call them for other work.

Personally, I have left the keys in my car, while it was running, 4 times! The local locksmith has devised a way so I do not forget to take the keys out of the ignition. If I do forget, they come right away to bail me out! They decided to give me a long red necklace to wear to hang my keys. They also hung a sign on my car door lock reminding me to take my keys out of the ignition!

Garage

The garage can be a haven for unwanted debris and junk. Before your tenants move in, remove anything that is not needed. I am a fanatic about not collecting things that you do not need. If there is no storage space in the garage, buy a simple shelving unit to avoid unwanted clutter. Keep only the tools or maintenance supplies that will be needed to continue the upkeep of the house.

One day a realtor asked me if she could store her sister's belongings in one of my garages. I said yes. After a year, the next tenant needed the room for storage, so I called the agent to have her remove her things. I had to call her many times before she finally removed her items.

Another time, I was nice again. I let one of my maintenance personnel store items in another garage. He told me it would be just for a month and only a few things. Well, guess what? This garage was full. The tenants complained, as he scattered debris and did not clean up after himself. I had to call him to remove the items, and I later found out that he lent this space to someone else for his or her clutter.

If the garage is freestanding, it must be maintained. Keep it freshly painted, remove any rotten wood, be sure the lock works on the door; tend to the roof if it needs repairs, and maintain the garage door opener. The shrubbery should be neatly trimmed around the garage.

A tenant will be more likely to keep the garage closed if it has an automatic garage door opener. This is especially true in bad weather. Your garage will be much drier and neater! Garage door openers can be fairly inexpensive, especially if you purchase more than one.

The garage door should be closed all the time so that the insects and animals do not build nests inside.

Windows

Because we have mainly old houses, the windows usually are the pull-string type and it is very hard to get them fixed. When the window is in really bad shape, it is better to completely change it.

Searching for a window company, I checked the newspaper and the yellow pages, and I got estimates from several companies. The estimates were outrageous, especially when they saw me, a woman. You can choose several types of windows, not welded or welded, bars or no bars, wooden or vinyl. I finally found a reputable window company. The windows are welded, and because they are rental houses, it can take more abuse. The price of the window, whether big or small, is the same. A basement window needs a slider to fit the exhaust of the drier.

In the long run, it is better to change the old or worn out windows because it will save on the heating bill!

I worked with one company who did not insulate, caulk or repair the trim. I called them about it and they said to ask my maintenance to do it. I will never trust him to do any of my work. Well, when I bought the ninth house, I needed fifty-three windows. Whom did I call? My favorite window company of course!

Roof

One of the most costly parts of the house to maintain is the roof. When I buy a house I want to make sure that the roof has a few more years left. I am still looking for a good roofer with reasonable prices. They are few and far between.

When I bought a house in the early years, I thought the roof was slate. Two years after I purchased the house, my painter told me that I had an asbestos roof. I called my brother, an architect in Maryland, to inquire about this type of roof. He told me to keep it because it will last for a long time, and change it only if it starts to leak. In the future, I would try to avoid this type of roof, because it would be costly to replace it, because there are various regulations regarding asbestos.

I did replace the roof right away on one house we purchased. I got such a good price on the house that it was worth spending the money on the repairs. This is one of the houses that I bought just before going to foreclosure.

A maintenance person inspects my roofs once or twice a year. I also do it when I frequently drive by. A window company representative who was installing windows noticed that the roof over the porch was sagging. This was an emergency, so I had one of my maintenance men support the roof before I can get estimates for the repair. I saw a carpenter near the house who was fixing a neighbor's siding. I asked him to take a look at the problem. He said that water damage was causing the roof to sag.

I had another incident with an early maintenance person, which ultimately cost me thousands of dollars. I saw a leak in the ceiling on the second floor one of the houses. I called the maintenance person to take a look and repair whatever needed to be done. He replaced some shingles. I discovered that he did not put flashing around the perimeter of the house and water leaked into the ceiling that covered the porch. The roof caved in. I learned my lesson and eventually hired a new maintenance person.

Attic

Since I have been working on the houses, I have never tried to go into an attic. I leave that responsibility to the maintenance person. I just make sure that we have enough insulation in the attic. However, one of my tenants called and she said that she could hear scratching on her ceiling. I had the same complaint about a year before and decided to call the pest control to come and check it out. They usually put bait in the attic and we have no problems after that.

We had another incident following this one; I called my pest control company and this time I ventured into the attic to see exactly what was going on. I saw a lot of debris and chewed cardboard, which meant there had been a squirrel living in the attic. We could also see a hole with daylight coming through into the attic. This was probably the source of the squirrel's entrance into the house.

I called a carpenter, who was recommended to me by my neighbor, to inspect this hole and repair it. He also repaired some of the floorboards. Now I am curious about all of my attics, and I intend to inspect them all.

This is another example that garbage is to be avoided around the perimeter of houses. I insist that barrels be covered at all times, and most of my tenants comply.

Basement

I just love the basement. As I mentioned earlier, it is the guts and the backbone of the house, and must be free of debris, junk, carton boxes, old paints, and the like. This could be turned into an extra recreation room for the house or storage area for the tenants.

When tenants leave, there are usually boxes, shoes, clothes, paper, furniture, and other things left in the basement. I have someone clean and throw out all items left by the tenant, and I charge the tenants if the place is left dirty and messy.

The clothes dryer should be vented outside properly, otherwise, there will be cobwebs all over the basement; cobwebs are fire hazards.

The washer and dryer in the basement should be cleaned thoroughly. Put lint from the dryer in the garbage can, and do not hang wet laundry in the basement. A basement is usually damp and cold, unless it has a special heating system, and wet clothes can cause mold. Ask your tenants to hang the clothes in the bathroom to dry.

HILDA'S HINT

Do not lend your basement or garage to friends or business associates to store their unwanted items. After all, if they are not using these items why do they need to store them?

I prefer a cemented basement. Some of them need to be redone, but this is costly. I am cementing each house, one at a time.

Another realtor used one of my basements to store her furniture. The tenants used her bed and TV, and lost her antique table. It was at her risk, and I told her this from the start.

Sump Pump

There were only two houses where we needed to install sump pumps. Basements tend to flood during heavy rains and snow in our area, and a sump pump is used to pump excess water from inside the basement or bottom floor.

When I saw one house and inspected the basement, I noticed water on the floor. I asked our maintenance person for advice and his answer was install a sump pump, and he did. The house was in good condition, so purchasing a sump pump did not hinder me from buying the house.

Landscaping

When I had only three houses, my maintenance personnel handled the landscaping and mowing the lawns. As I acquired more houses, I hired a landscaper to do all of the outside maintenance on the lawns and shrubbery. He does a beautiful job with the lawns and keeps the hedges trimmed as well. I have another person who maintains the hedges on one of the houses. The landscaper also pitches in to help me move furniture when I need him.

HILDA'S HINT

Avoid planting near the foundation of the house, as the roots may grow into it and disturb it.

When we need to put in some flowering bushes, I purchase them at the local nursery and have them delivered. We keep the bushes trimmed and fertilized, and put lime on the grass.

Driveways

Each house has an asphalt driveway except for one, which is cement. The only reason this house has a cement driveway is because the asphalt company could not get their truck through the six foot wide leeway.

I had a problem with one of the asphalt driveways. The driveways were cracked and when it rained, water was seeped through the basement! I telephoned a company and the technician came to the house to see the problem. I told him it appeared that the driveway needed to be sealed and hot asphalt needed to be put in the cracks. Well, immediately his estimate rose $1500, as he figured he was dealing with someone who did not know what they were talking about! This happens quite often with me. Service technicians or vendors will see they are dealing with a woman, and try to take advantage of me. They soon find out that I have knowledge and expertise, and they begin to treat me fairly.

I was driving around Newport following the episode with the driveway, and I made the "Discovery of the Day!" I noticed a truck doing some work on the big shopping mall. They were sealing the driveway and putting hot asphalt in the cracks. I approached the truck and asked for the company's business card. I gave the technician my card and he went to my houses and gave me an estimate for repairing the driveways. This estimate was $235 as compared with the previous estimate of $1500.00!

They arrived to do the work and my maintenance personnel had roped off the driveways and asked the tenants to leave their cars in the streets. It is not the responsibility of the asphalt company to wake up my tenants so that they can move their cars and he can complete his job. They did a beautiful job!

Porches

Some of my houses have covered porches, which require less maintenance work. The uncovered porches need a lot of work, although they look so much nicer and are very relaxing to sit on and enjoy life. This is especially true in the houses close to the water. Six of the houses have uncovered porches, and it seems that the paint is always peeling on them. It looks terrible! I asked my floor service technician if he could sand and stain them, rather than paint them. He did this to a few of the porches, but after some time I saw the wood bleeding through the stain. I called my maintenance person and showed him what was happening. He said that they should have put a primer coat on first, then the stain. This would have avoided the wood bleeding. We will wait until spring to buff it and apply primer and then another coat of stain.

Another local hardware store representative showed me Cabot stain when I told him about the bleeding problem. He showed me the solution of preventing the wood from bleeding. Put primer on first, then the Cabot stain. This provides excellent resistance to extractive bleeding, mildew and moisture. Then, apply the solid color deck stain.

Exterior Painting/Aluminum/Vinyl Siding

Painting the exterior or installing aluminum or vinyl siding are costly maintenance projects for any house. I have four houses with vinyl or aluminum siding and my two duplexes have clapboard on the outside. They all need maintenance. I got estimates for the exterior painting, plus some repairs of the rotten wood and the vinyl siding. If there is small difference in the prices of painting versus vinyl siding, I definitely put on the vinyl siding. It lasts longer, while painting has to be re-done approximately every five years.

Estimates for painting depend on what type of paint is used. Obviously, if a lower quality paint is used it will be less costly. I want the job to be done the right way, to look nice and last me a few years.

I received the two estimates, with a difference of almost $10,000. When I saw these estimates, I decided that I needed to apply for a home equity loan so I can pay the repairs in installments. I am now in search of a bank that will give me a home equity loan. Since my properties are held in an LLC, it is more difficult to obtain a loan. Although if the bank sees that I own a small business, I should be able to get the loan with a secured asset on the property. I am estimating this job to be completed in shortly. I have chosen gray as the background of the house and the shutters will be maroon.

HILDA'S HINT

Do not wait to call a gutter cleaner until the last minute. Sometimes it can take months to fit you in their schedule. Everyone wants his gutters cleaned before the bad weather. Find a reliable person and make an annual schedule for cleanings. You will save a lot of money in repairs by having your gutters cleaned regularly.

Gutter

I have the maintenance person check the gutters and downspouts for clogs, and clean them periodically, to keep the leaves, twigs and other outside matter away. If the gutters are not cleaned, it can cause damage. Clean gutters help to prevent leaks on the roof, moss on the sidings, and flooding in the basement.

One day as I was looking through the local yellow pages, I saw an advertisement for a gutter cleaner. I called, and he is fantastic. He cleans and repairs the gutters and down spouts. This is one maintenance issue that no longer worries me. We have scheduled periodic cleanings and I am very satisfied. He always notifies me prior to doing the jobs.

Flower Boxes

I always admired the flower boxes around Newport restaurants and the various bed and breakfast Inns. I put some boxes on the outside of several houses, but they never bloomed as beautifully. I live one hour away and I could not maintain them properly. I had someone who was supposed to take care of them, keep them watered, fertilized and change the flowers, but it did not work out.

I asked around at the flower garden shop if they knew anyone to handle this project and they did not. Finally, I met the salesman from the local hardware store while I was buying some impatiens, and I asked him if he knew anyone who could do it. He recommended a flower design company. I met with the owner, to discuss what I wanted. She added a few more boxes, and told me I was very easy to please! The houses are close to where she works, so it was not a problem. City Hall hires her company to do the plants and flowers all around Newport. She is very talented and well known in this area.

HILDA'S HINT

The added touch of flowers, shrubbery or small trees in the yards will add beauty to the house, and value!

The boxes are gorgeous! When I saw them I left a message on the owner's answering machine about how I much I appreciated her work. One of my tenants almost cried when she saw them.

Chimney/Fireplace

Since purchasing my houses, I have never had the chimneys cleaned. About a year ago my maintenance personnel in charge of the boilers and air-conditioners mentioned that I should have the ductwork checked in my primary residence, as it may need cleaning. During the cleaning we learned that the filters were very dirty and that they should be replaced four times per year. We used a company called Air Duct. I asked them if they would travel to Newport. They came and assessed our situation with all of our houses. They cleaned and vacuumed all of the chimneys in our Newport houses and, now maintain them every two years.

We have four fireplaces in three different houses. Some of the fireplaces have been covered up in the other houses. At some point, I would like to locate the original fireplaces in the houses.

Plumbing

Since I started buying houses, I went through several plumbers before I found a good one.

One plumber did not cut the ceiling to repair a leak. He told me to get a carpenter to do it and he would come back. I had another plumber give me an estimate and he was able to do the entire job.

There was that one plumber who screamed at me when the payment was not made in cash. I usually pay by check for accounting purposes and we need to give a 1099 form if the job exceeds $600. There was another plumber who changed the hardware of the shower, and forgot to re-connect the pipe. When the tenant took a shower all the water came down to the second floor.

Now, I have a regular plumber who takes care of all of the plumbing needs of the houses and coordinates them with our maintenance person. When we bought the ninth house, he changed the hardware of the plumbing system, because it was rusty. I can depend on the plumber to let me know what work needs to be completed, and can trust him to handle the job professionally.

HILDA'S HINT

> It is fine to get estimates from more than one service vendor. Again, my rule of thumb is the cheapest may not always be the best man or woman for the job!

I also call Roto-Rooter regularly. They are easily accessible and always come immediately when I have a problem. They have a fixed price for a service call and repairs, and they will usually give me a discount.

Electrical

I often ask my realtor to give me a name of a good service provider. I needed the name of an electrician, I really struck gold! I have a wonderful local company doing all of my electrical work. He has a fax and a cellular phone, which are essential in doing business these days. I will call him if I need any thing done at the houses. I ask when he is available and we make an appointment for a date and time. I then inform the tenants when he will arrive. When I buy a house, I tell the electrician at least two months before closing, and let him know exactly what work will need to be done. He always gives me the time, right away.

We usually have 150-200 amperage in the houses. With one house, there was a short circuit in the electrical system all the time. The maintenance person discovered it when the tenants used their hair drier and it always happened. My electrician rewired the two bathrooms for the hair drier, and since then we have not had any trouble.

Heater/Boiler/Water Heater

All of my properties are oil heated, except for the condominium. I found a local oil company that I consistently use. Since the gas company cut down a lot of their services, it is not convenient to do business with them for several houses. The gas company had serviced the condominium since 1980, and suddenly the technician said that they could not give us a service contract. My regular oil company recommended another company who services the gas heater.

When I inspect a house, the heating system is a top priority. When the boiler is aging, I usually change it. My oil company has all of the plans that I need. They will do a three-year financing, which is easier to pay and I can give a down payment and get reasonable rates. I have done several houses with them. When they did the ninth house, they left a mess in the basement. This had never happened before, and they will never hear the end of this! They cleaned up their mess immediately and I read them the riot act. There was no excuse for this. They gave me free, one-year maintenance service after they installed the new boilers.

HILDA'S HINT

If you are not satisfied with service or a job completed at your house, complaining or screaming at the service technician is not always recommended. However, venting your frustration can sometimes get the job done properly, and it sure makes you feel a whole lot better!!

I get maintenance contracts for all of the houses with 24-hour service, so the tenants do not have to wait till the next day without heat and hot water. The boiler is cleaned once a year.

Sometime in November I ask the tenants and the oil company to test the heating systems, giving us time to take care of any repairs and replace filters, before the cold weather comes.

Now that I am familiar with the different size water heaters, I buy the seventy-nine gallon water heaters because I do not like to hear tenants complaining about not having enough hot water.

Each room should have a heater. The ninth house did not have a heater on the third floor and in the kitchen on the second floor, so I had the oil company install new ones.

Air-conditioning Units

The only air-conditioned place I have is in the condominium. A technician from a local company maintains the heating and air-conditioning in this unit, and he also does my primary house, coming twice a year for maintenance.

It is essential to keep air-conditioning ducts clean and free from debris. This helps the system last longer, and keeps allergens and dust from entering the house through the ducts.

Telephone

I have a local telephone man who does all of the inside wiring for the telephones in each house. It depends how many lines the tenants need. We usually have three lines in each house. Sometimes, they need only one line, because they have cellular phones. Most of the college students like to have their own line for their computers.

It is the tenants responsibility to contact the telephone company for phone numbers, which must be turned on before the line can be hooked up to their respective rooms or wherever they want them to be.

I am in control of the wiring and phone lines, because I do not want additional holes in the walls. Tenants notify me of their desires, and I have my regular phone man do the installations. I use only one person for this job, because he is familiar with the houses and my wishes.

Cable

Most tenants like to have cable television. If there is no hook-up, I give permission for the cable man to put holes on the walls. Now, tenants can subscribe to telephone and cable from one company, which makes things much easier.

Our telephone man also does the inside wiring for the cable.

Dehumidifier

I noticed that basements were stuffy smelling. I bought nine dehumidifiers from a local appliance store and had them delivered to each house, installed where possible, and I had my maintenance man do the rest. I ordered the maximum capacity for all except two of the houses, where the basements are smaller.

We make sure the flow of water goes to the drain in the basement, if it has one, to prevent the floor from becoming wet.

Dehumidifiers are some of the best investments I have made. They save our basements and make them smell nicer, and they will also save our foundations from drying up.

Garbage Collection

I usually have four or five forty-gallon plastic covered containers for the garbage, along with two recycling bins at each house. The tenants are responsible for putting them out on collection days. I provide them with a pick-up schedule. Some tenants sometimes forget, so I have assigned someone to make sure the containers are placed at the curb and garbage is not scattered around the neighborhood.

If at the end of a lease there is too much debris left at the house, I have our lawn maintenance man take it to the dump. This costs money therefore I will charge the tenants.

Our new maintenance person showed me how to deal with leftover debris at no cost. The city will collect everything. You must notify them of large items

HILDA'S HINT

Providing the house with bins, the trash pick-up schedule and information on recycling, will help to keep unwanted pests and rodents away from the house.

to be picked up, and cut and tie the cardboard according to regulations. They will not pick up anything if the pick-up rules have not been followed. This man is now in charge of this task. I am happy that the problem got solved, and we no longer have to pay to dump the debris.

Pest Control

For twenty-five years, I have had a local pest control company maintain my personal home's pest control on a quarterly basis. I have contracts with them for our Newport houses. They invoice me quarterly, I pay them once per year and they are happy.

When a house has a pest problem, the company sends someone immediately to take care of it. Once, one of my carpenters saw a squirrel in the house. As we must respect animal rights, they made sure when the squirrel came out, we just plugged the hole. If we have problem with birds, we call the wild life refuge.

When the pest control technician sees that a tenant's kitchen is a total mess, with scattered food, an uncovered garbage can, or that there is trash thrown in the yard, he will immediately contact me. I make sure that the tenants clean up or I will hire somebody to do the work and the tenants will pay.

The pest control technician does not want to reveal his cellular phone number. He feels that if his customers have this number, he will be deluged with phone calls. He told me that if I have a problem to call the main office, leave a message and they would contact him. Sometimes when I leave a message they do not return my call for several days. Why leave a message? I called the managers of the pest control company and told them that I did not intend to gossip and chitchat with the technician I am busy enough! I have been dealing with this company for twenty-five years and they would be out of their minds not to give me his telephone number. One of the managers called and gave me the cellular phone number. Shortly after, I saw some bees nests in three of our houses. I called the technician and he came right away!

Smoke Alarms/Fire Extinguishers/Fire Ladders

Once I called the Newport fire department chief to ask him to recommend someone to check the houses twice a year for fire safety. He gave me a name of a man who lives in the same neighborhood as one of my rental houses, a former fire chief of Newport with over forty years experience. I said, "He is my neighbor," and checked the telephone directory for his number. Now he oversees all of my houses. He checks them when we change to daylight savings time, so it is easier to remember.

HILDA'S HINT

Having your local fire department check your fire extinguishers and smoke detectors bi-annually can also teach your tenants about fire safety. This will show them that you care about their safety as well as the houses. They will thank you for it!

What made me think of having the fire department check all of my houses? Whenever tenants leave, the cleaners always see that the smoke alarms are disconnected and hanging down from the ceiling .The tenants use the batteries for their radios or Walkmans. If someone smokes in the house, the alarm makes a noise, so they will often remove the battery.

We always put a small fire extinguisher in every kitchen. When we have a third floor in a house, we also provide a fire ladder.

I give a form to the tenants when the fire maintenance man checks the houses.

Maintenance Cleaning

After cleaning the condominium by myself for fourteen years, I needed to get help to clean the houses. Again, the realtors were my referral source for finding personnel. I started out with two to three groups of house cleaners to take care of the houses when tenants moved out. I like having a few groups, so if one group is busy then another group would take over, especially on short notice. When I looked at what the groups were being paid, it was not enough to encourage them to stay under my employ. I could not keep them busy enough, and they all wanted more work.

It is hard to find someone reliable. I finally found someone who is not only reliable but also trustworthy, and serious about what she does. I chose her to be in charge of the interior cleaning of all of my houses. If she cannot handle the cleaning workload, she gets help from friends and I pay them separately. She has another full time job, as I keep her busy only during the summer.

I make a schedule for the head of the cleaning crew for the upcoming year so she will know when she needs help. The cleaning days are all highlighted in pink. She appreciates the fact that I am very organized and can plan so far ahead. She usually has a man clean the basement and the cobwebs from the rafters.

Maintenance cleaning is imperative for us, as it helps with the upkeep of the house. I usually ask the realtor to include a clause in the lease about cleaning. We have cleaning women, who can clean once a week for a small fee, including the bathrooms, kitchen, living room, hallway, but not the individual bedrooms. The women will vacuum the bedrooms if clothes and junk are not scattered on the floor. If the tenants do not have the house periodically cleaned, I will charge them when they leave. The house is usually in pretty bad condition if the cleaning has not been done. There are exceptions. Some groups are so clean that I am shocked when I see the house on moving day.

HILDA'S HINT

Be sure to tell your tenants how pleased you are that they took the time to care for your house. These are the types of tenants you want to rent your house.

Laundry

Linens and towels are provided for the summer tenants or for short rentals for the regatta crew. When we had only two houses we just did the laundry in the washers and dryers in the houses. Now that we have more houses, I found a Laundromat to do our linens.

The closer the Laundromat is to the center of town, the higher the price per pound ($/lb). I went to several places out of town and found the Laundromat very reasonable in price. I deal with the woman in charge, who now knows the routine. My cleaning crew chief brings the laundry, specifies which house it belongs to and then picks it up later. I receive a phone call to let me know how much I owe. We have been with this service for over five years.

Linens/Towels/Comforters/Pillows

A furnished house must include bed linens, towels, and pillows. With one or two houses this is not a problem. I devised a simple system to keep myself sane! Thank you for the "Bed-in-a-Bag" ensemble. Each house has one kind of print, so we know which print belongs to which house. The actual linens are not labeled, but I have a log sheet to keep track of patterns and colors. I try to purchase current patterns, to keep with style and to avoid problems finding replacements when needed.

We provide six towels of one color per bathroom in each house. I purchased eighteen towels per color, as each house has at least two bathrooms. What fun I had shopping for those!

We have two pillows per full-size bed, each with a pillow protector. Sometimes a tenant will request one or two more pillows.

HILDA'S HINT

The best place to buy bedding linens and towels are the factory outlets or discount stores. Donate any worn items to your local charity or church for their bazaar.

If I have college students or Navy officers renting, they provide their own towels and linens. After the summer season, where in the world would I store all these towels and linens? One of the houses has a big basement with plenty of storage space. I ordered more than twenty-five sixty-gallon plastic stackable containers, and label them with the contents and house address. We also insert a laundry freshener in the container. We tried to put them in each house, but sometimes the tenants open them and use them.

Floors

When I saw House #2, the carpet looked good, so I did not replace it. We inspected all rooms with carpet to make sure there were hardwood floors underneath. When the owner moved out, I saw the carpet in the living room was all faded and worn, and I decided to replace the carpet and sand the floors. One bedroom on the second floor also had carpet that was glued to the floor. My maintenance person gave me an estimate to sand the living room and the bedroom floors, which came out perfect. The third floor had area carpet and the floors were painted on the perimeter, so we did not touch them.

House #7's floors needed sanding. As soon as we had a week to fix the floor, we sanded two rooms. This time, I had another maintenance person to do the job. We rented the machines and sand paper. It came out nice, although it was more hassle to rent the equipment and do it ourselves.

Because the houses are old, the floors were primarily hardwood. As soon as I closed on one house, we removed the carpet and sanded it. It is better in terms of cleanliness to have hardwood floors although it is more expensive to do the sanding. In the long run, it is more expensive when you steam clean the carpet every time a tenant leaves the unit.

I found another wonderful local floor company. They are excellent in their trade! I like their oil base stain. It lasts longer and can withstand heavy traffic. When the contract says the closets are included, they do it. He did the floors at two of my houses. House #9 has three floors, and he did a beautiful job on the floors and the closets. The floors on the third floor were all painted, and the paint preserved them very well.

HILDA'S HINT

You may think you will save money by doing some repairs yourself. Remember your time is money! Hire a professional. This will ensure that the job is done to code, and you will be able to spend your time handling other necessities.

Because of their excellent work, I asked them to do the porch at my residence, as the paint was peeling after a previous painter had painted it. When they knew that the weather would be good for a few days, they said, " We are doing Hilda's porch." This was another superior job well done! Now they do all of the porches in Newport, when the weather forecast is sunny for several consecutive days.

In consideration, I always make sure that I call the company to schedule the work well in advance.

Interior Painting

When painting House #1, I used semi-gloss white paint. I have now changed my mind since my favorite painter painted # 6 and # 7 houses. I recognize and believe now that painting a house is not just a job. A painter is an artist. His choice of color makes the house look elegant. It is too bad that he lives far from Newport, but I have learned a valuable lesson from him. It is not just the color, but also the technique of using gloss, semi-gloss or flat paints give various appearances to a room.

I have learned how to accent walls with different colors. When I go inside a house, it makes me feel good when the place is beautiful. I have received several comments from the neighbors that I did a beautiful job on the house.

I purchase my paints from Sherwin Williams and Pittsburgh Paints at my local hardware store.

Sherwin Williams keeps a record of the paints we use in each house and they give me a computerized printout for each. It is so easy, and I do not get confused. I decided to use Pittsburgh Paints for some of the houses. They have a chart of three choices of different hue colors, making it much easier to decide colors, when you can see the three already blended together for the walls, the trim and the accents.

I have three maintenance people to paint my houses. One of them called to say that I should first look at the bathroom in one of the houses, to see if the paint colors were appealing. He was right and we made some changes. Another maintenance person also did the same thing when he called me to check the paint.

This was the first time we tried to use the paint combinations with the chart from Pittsburgh Paints. The third house was all painted and I was not called to check on the color, after a portion was painted. I made a comment, "I think the colors are not as cool and appealing as the other house." The maintenance person responded, "You chose the color and not me." As soon as I entered the house, I saw part of the wall that went up the stairs, was not caulked. It destroyed the look of this entire part of the wall. I am a fanatic about caulking. He also did not sand one portion of the door, and just painted over it. Aside from these two spots, the paint job was beautiful, especially the kitchen and the bathroom.

HILDA'S HINT

Using a semi-gloss paint makes cleaning dirt from the walls a much easier job.

I had a bad experience with one group of painters. They were very messy and there was paint everywhere on the floor and carpets. I did not hire them again.

Bathrooms

Bathrooms are one of the most expensive rooms to repair. When I buy a house I want to make sure that it has at least two bathrooms. To save the tiles, we caulk them to prevent leakage. If there is leakage, it can destroy the ceiling and that is another huge problem. I make sure that we caulk the bathrooms each time somebody leaves the unit. There is usually mold in the shower and the bathtub. Mold grows when the bathroom is not properly cleaned. When one stays in the unit for six months and does not clean for their duration of their lease, we have problem.

There are new 1.5-gallon toilets that are water savers. When it is time to change the toilet, we now purchase these. We have a few spare toilets in our inventory. If a toilet breaks at night or on a weekend, we are covered.

Shower curtains are also important. I usually buy a fabric shower curtain, because you can wash it in the washing machine. It is important to get water and mold resistant fabric. In several of the houses we have old-fashioned claw foot bathtubs. I bought three shower curtains of the same design for each, and had them sewn together. This enclosed the entire shower and prevented any water spillage on the floor and the back wall.

HILDA'S HINT

If you have multiple houses it is important to keep an inventory of items for emergencies. When buying replacement items, buy an extra one or two. Ask your store for a multiple item discount, especially on larger items. You will be surprised at the money you will save in time.

You need an exhaust system in a bathroom to avoid paint peeling. The steam will cause peeling paint. If the paint job is not prepared right, it can also peel.

Medicine cabinets tend to rust and need to be changed. I saw a sale at Home Depot on medicine cabinets for half price. I bought six along with some other bathroom inventory items, and had them delivered.

Kitchen

After purchasing nine houses, I have not had to remodel any of the kitchens, which can be a huge expense. When I initially purchase a house, I am sure that the kitchen does not need of major repairs. I may paint the cabinets or replace the linoleum floor, but that is the extent of it. If a house does not have a dishwasher, I install one. A dishwasher is essential in my book!! If we need some additional kitchen cabinets, I go to Home Depot and purchase some.

HILDA'S HINT

You can purchase inexpensive kitchen items and gadgets at local department stores such as Wal-Mart or K-Mart or The Christmas Tree Shoppe. You can usually get some great buys, especially if you purchase in bulk

Kitchen Wares and Gadgets

I provide all of the kitchen wares including dishes, drinking glasses, pots and pans, coffee maker, toaster, can opener, set of knives, silverware and basic cooking utensils. The cleaning group informs me when it is time to replace or purchase new kitchen items. I also provide a wastebasket for each room in the house, a garbage container for the kitchen and a can for the rubbish to be placed outside.

Appliances

For twenty years I purchased my appliances from a store near my house. They were willing to deliver if I bought more appliances, but when I ordered just one, I got a sermon from the owner. Well, I found a good and reliable store in Newport. When I buy a house, this store is another one to call on my list for appliance estimates. They have a very good and reliable repair service. I supply their telephone number to tenants in case they need appliance repairs.

I supply a washer and dryer for each house, not coin operated. Tenants pay good money and utilities with a cap, so this is one convenience that I give to them.

When I buy a house, the refrigerator usually goes with the sale. With the first sign of needing repair, I usually buy new ones with at least eighteen cubic feet of space.

I purchase electric ranges for all of the houses. They are easier to maintain. Some of the houses have the exhaust systems vented outside and some do not. I am in the process of converting all of the exhaust hood systems to vent outside for safety. Each hood has a filter and I make sure they are changed two or three times per year, as part of our annual winter inspection.

Every house has a dishwasher. If I have to replace an old dishwasher, I purchase a 'quiet' model.

I also supply a microwave for each house. The wattage of each should be at least 600-1000 watts, otherwise they wear out quickly. I ask the tenants to use the range to cook instead of the microwave, which should be for re-heating or quick meals.

Not every house has a garbage disposal. The plumber and the maintenance person advised me not to install them. It seems that garbage disposals are the #1 appliance needing repairs. They get clogged with anything you can think of including spoons, bottle caps, coins, pieces of glass and much much more!

I supply an iron and ironing board for each house. I make sure that I purchase an iron that has an automatic shut-off switch, for safety reasons. I also purchase a standard sized ironing board, not a tabletop model or small one.

After I bought the first two houses, I bought vacuum cleaners on sale. When buying replacement bags, I had no problems because I could remember the bag size of the vacuum. With more houses, it is a big problem. Since I purchase sale vacuums, they are not always the same brand and model; therefore the size of the bag differs. The tenants do not change the bags when they are full and the vacuums get ruined. They can buy refills in the grocery store, but I think they just do not think about it.

Solving my problem, Wal-Mart had a spring sale of vacuum cleaners, $49 each, so I bought three packs of bags, size 2, with each machine. I ordered twelve and thirty-six packs of bags. The person in-charge of the vacuum department that day was thrilled!

HILDA'S HINT

If you have multiple houses, purchase similar items for each. This way, you can switch items if necessary and use their parts, and you will not have to stand in the department store with a perplexed look on your face when trying to buy replacement pieces!

Picture Frames

There are so many walls and they are all painted. How will you save the walls from getting beaten up? Put up pictures!

The young Navy officers have some artwork with them and they like their rooms to be comfortable like at home. The college students want something more current like group singers and actors. I told the college students that if they want to hang extra pictures I would ask my maintenance man to put them up. He knows where the studs are in the walls, so the pictures will not fall and cause damage. If they tape anything to the walls and remove it when they leave, I will charge them to repair the peeling paint.

Where do I buy these pictures? You can go to the factory outlets and to K-Mart, Michael's Craft, and Building 19 1/9. When I travel I also like to pick up three or four pictures from the places and countries that I visit.

When the tenants put too many holes in the walls, I charge them. Tenants can put up their own pictures as long as they use the existing nail holes. If they take down the frames on the wall and store them, they must be in the same place as when they removed them and not damaged, or I will charge them.

Window Treatments

Whenever I inspect a house, the first thing I ask is, "Are the window treatments included in the sale?" The curtains and blinds are usually left in the house.

When I bought the first house, I went to the Country Curtain in Garden City in Cranston, Rhode Island, to purchase window treatments. I bought a complete set of curtains for each window. The windows had pull-down shades, which were in good condition, so I did not need to change them. The bill for the curtains was high. I needed to find a place to purchase quality window treatments for less money. Was I thrilled when I discovered the factory outlets!

A friend showed me the local curtain outlet in Northbridge, Massachusetts. I met the manager and asked her to help me choose some curtains for another house. She showed me a few sets of curtains for House #6. I liked what she showed me so much, that I bought forty-three sets for the house, which is a duplex. If you buy quality materials, they will last longer. This store buys overstocks from bigger companies. I specify to the manager if the items are for the bedrooms, bathroom, kitchen, hallways and the like, and how many I need for each room.

HILDA'S HINT

Keep a log of the stores from which you purchase items. Indicate the salesperson's name, the phone number and address of the store, and what items you purchased, and the prices. This is a good reference when you need to purchase replacements, and also good for comparison-shopping!

In another house I purchased, all the shades were torn and I discovered that I could use valances and darkening blinds. I did not have to buy curtain sets. Well, one of our maintenance personnel measured the windows and ordered the blinds from Home Depot. I called the curtain factory outlet store and asked the manager to watch for some good buys for twenty-three windows. She found one, called me and we purchased them. When they were installed, they looked very nice.

Carpet

The only unit that I own that has wall-to-wall carpet is the condominium. The carpet lasted a long time, fifteen years. I steam clean once or twice a year when each tenant leaves. The condo was brand new when we bought it and we were able to choose the carpeting. I just changed it recently and I still do the steam cleaning regularly.

Since the houses mainly have hardwood floors, I usually accent the houses with area rugs. I have the owner of a local carpet cleaning company pick up and clean the area rugs when the tenants leave. I schedule the appointments as soon as I know the date the tenants are moving out.

When I bought House #9 I discovered that my neighbor, has a carpet cleaning service. I have searched for a good and reasonable carpeting store and have finally found one!

Furniture

All of my houses are furnished making them easier to rent. When I first started, I went to a thrift shop to look at furniture, through the recommendation of a realtor. I bought something, but they were not able to supply enough furniture for all the houses, so I had to look for another alternative.

I went to a furniture store in Blackstone, Massachusetts, and I bought enough furnishing for all the houses. He gave me a break on the prices, and I paid in installments.

For each house, I provide double size beds, a living room and a dining room set, dressers and night tables, entertainment center and tables. Depending on the size of the house, the furniture sizes and styles vary. When I purchase dressers for the bedrooms, I try to keep the same style model for each house. The only time I provide twin beds are when a full size bed cannot fit through the door. The movers sometimes use the windows to bring the furniture to the third floor of a house.

I discovered another local furniture dealer when I saw that they had advertised a two-year no interest payment plan for furniture. I had to find out what "no interest" meant. The company absorbs the interest from the bank if you pay the invoice in monthly installments prior to the agreed upon date. The other furniture store told me that I would be charged in some hidden way. The salesman at the original furniture store explained the way it worked. I tried it and it worked exactly that way.

I work with a very nice salesman. He is a mild mannered, courteous and very efficient salesman. Now before I buy a house, the salesman gives me an estimate of the price of the furniture I am interested in and when the ad comes up I order it. They are very efficient and the delivery is flexible. I tell them when the house will be ready and they always deliver right on time. During the day of the delivery, I give them instructions to call me on my cellular phone (a blessing we have them) one hour before they arrive, so that I can do other work and not just wait for them in the house.

This store also has a service called "Dr. Furniture." If something gets damaged they will fix it for free. Dr. Furniture will go to the house and if the item cannot be fixed, a delivery truck will pick it up. I just became aware that I have a two-year warranty to fix any purchased furniture. I need to discuss what happens after the warranty expires with the president of the company. If I do not get satisfaction or answers, I always go to the top! One day I happened to meet the President of the furniture store and I mentioned the past warranties, and that I did not like it that his company gave me a hard time when I inquired about warranties when I needed the furniture repaired. He said to tell the salesman and he would take care of it. No wonder this man is so successful in his business. He takes very good care of his customers!

HILDA'S HINT

Check out all types of stores when looking for furniture. Used furniture is not always the most economical way to go. Buying new furniture is a better investment. It will last longer and need fewer repairs.

At the end of the summer, I evaluate the need to change the furniture. It is better to buy new furniture when the fabric fades or gets worn. It is not a good idea to re-upholster because sometimes the foam is sagging and it will cost more money to do it. And used furniture stores do not have "interest free for two-years!" Old furniture can be given to charity or to a church.

WICKER CHAIRS

I have a set of wicker chairs that I inherited from one of the previous homeowners. They are a costly set needing some repair work. I called one person who had advertised in the newspaper who told me that the chairs could not be repaired. He said, "If you are throwing them away, I will take them from you." I realized that something was wrong. He is telling me they are not any good, yet wants them. Hmmm... I did not call him back. I am from the Philippines, where I know that anything can be fixed.

I had a painter put a coat of paint on them, but the paint kept peeling and falling off. They looked awful. The painter did not know how to properly prepare the chairs.

One day I was reading the newspaper and there was another advertisement from a local upholsterer, saying he could repair wicker chairs and I called him. The owner told me that he had been repairing wicker chairs for the Newport Mansions for a long time, so I commissioned him to do the job. After working on one of the chairs, I could tell that he really knew how to handle them. He fixed the broken ones and told me that these are "the real thing." They are truly antique wicker chairs. That is why the first repairman wanted me to give him the chairs. He knew what I had.

This set has six chairs, a love seat, a lounge chair and a flowerbox. For my other front porches, I buy the resin style wicker furniture because it can withstand more abuse. I am having the "wicker man" work on some of my other furniture for repairs. I have given him two sofas that need upholstering, as well as a dresser that needs to be repaired. All are oak and worth restoring to their original beauty.

My tenants love the little added extras of wicker furniture on their front porches. They appreciate that I take time to purchase these items that will truly make them feel like they are at home.

Suppliers

My best supplier for general household items is a local hardware store. As I was buying a lock for one of the houses, I saw that my local store had a sign on the picnic table, "We Will Deliver!" I spoke with the owner, and asked him if they can deliver other items like garbage barrels. He immediately said "yes." They deliver! I could not believe that I found such a store. I have a small car, a Subaru Impreza. I could not fit ten forty-gallon barrels in my car. They were willing to deliver and even put the address on each barrel for each house. I will be buying paint there from now on.

HILDA'S HINT

Sometimes your local stores will be your best suppliers. They will go the extra mile to provide customer service and to please you. Ask if they deliver. If you are a good customer, they will do anything to make you happy and encourage you to come back and shop in their store.

Home Depot is another supplier that also delivers. You can buy anything from them, like bathroom fixtures, cabinets, bulbs, hoses and carpet. I have also discovered another local store. The toilet sets are complete and come in one box, including paraffin seals. At Home Depot, it is separate. I have learned something about toilet structure.

After completing some of these projects myself, I believe that I am qualified for other degrees from Home Depot University or from Wal-Mart University!

CHAPTER 5 Renting

Finding the Perfect Tenants

There are many types of tenants: good, bad, acceptable, long-term, short-term, perfect and those who are just "good-enough!" I would like to tell you that every tenant I have chosen was perfect, but that certainly is not the case. Living in a resort area, I mainly rent to summer vacationers, Navy officers, college students and families. I have rented to quite a mix of people, who for the most part have been very nice and responsible.

If I am working with a summer rental, I want a mature and quiet group of people. If they invite the entire state of Massachusetts that are noisy, I do not want them in one of my houses. Do not get me wrong there are many good renters from Massachusetts, but the proximity to Newport is about 1 1/2 hours. Friends or family can easily make the drive for a long weekend to see the tenants.

I usually have no problems with the military renters. They are very easy to deal with and most accommodating. The college students on the other hand, are a different story.

I learned the hard way when it comes to renting to college students. I experimented with different age groups and weeded out the ones that cause problems. One realtor showed a house to a group of young college students. They loved it and were interested in renting. It was now my turn to interview them. I adamantly told them that I do not tolerate loud parties. I informed the Newport police that they should cite them on their first offense, and that my lawyer would pursue the quick eviction notice which is in effect in Newport.

If the group really likes the house and they realize that I mean what I said, they will usually rent the house. One summer I was referred to a group of vacationers for a summer rental. As always, I informed the prospective tenants of the rules and regulations. They did not want to be bothered with the city's rules, the neighborhood rules, and my rules. I told the realtor to find another house for them to rent.

The realtor will assess the prospective tenants using my guidelines and other basic questions. They will then determine if the applicants will abide by the city's rules as well as mine.

Tenant selection needs to be done carefully. You have the right to be "picky" as this is your property, and in my case, since my houses are furnished, these are my belongings. Listed below are the most popular ways of finding tenants:

Classified Newspaper Ads

"For Rent" sign displayed in the front of the house

Personal Referrals

Real Estate Agents

Classified Newspaper Advertising

Classified newspaper advertising seems to be the most popular method of finding prospective tenants. There is a fee for placing the ad, and you as the landlord will get an overabundance of telephone calls from people who are "just looking." Classified ads will certainly reach the most people, if the newspaper has a wide circulation. You will need to put information in your ad to attract tenants, and also to screen out inappropriate tenants. **For example:**

4 BR/2.5 BA house,
nice yard, N/P, $1000 mo.

This ad will definitely save you money on the placement costs, but you will get every person under the sun calling you, asking questions. Include more information in your ad, to screen callers. If a prospective tenant does not like what he sees, he will skip over your ad, and you will only get phone calls from seriously interested renters. The ad should read:

> **4 BR/2.5 BA house- fenced yard,**
> **near schools & shopping,**
> **FP, pool, N/P, N/S, 1 1/2 mo.**
> **security, $1000 mo.**

Including information such as "near schools & shopping, fireplace, swimming pool, no pets, no smoking," and the amount of the security deposit required, will help qualify your house for renters.

"For Rent" Sign

Putting a "For Rent" sign in the front window of the house or on the front lawn is tricky. I would not recommend this unless you are in large development or on a busy street. It tells all prospective renters that the house is available for rent, and it does not give any other information. Therefore, you will get many phone calls from renters who may not meet your requirements. On the flip side, putting up a "For Rent" may work to your advantage. Someone may be driving home from work, need a place to rent, see the sign and call. This could be your ideal renter, although the chances are very remote.

HILDA'S HINT

If you are aware that a renter will not be renewing the lease, you may want to pass out a flyer to the neighbors alerting them of the house availability. Neighbors will usually recommend a friend or relative, because they want to keep the neighborhood friendly and close.

Personal Referrals

A renter referral from an existing renter, friend or neighbor is another way of finding people. I am leery of an existing renter recommending someone, especially if they are breaking the lease. Unless there are extenuating circumstances, when someone has to break a lease and recommends a friend to assume the lease, you will need to do a credit check on the friend. Tenant screening will be covered later in this chapter.

Since I rent to military personnel, they sometimes get transferred on short notice. They will refer me to other military personnel, usually works out fine.

Real Estate Agent Referrals

Using a realtor to find tenants is the best and most economical way for me. There are real estate agents that just sell, some that just rent, and others who handle both. I prefer the agent that just rents or rents/sells. An agent who rents my houses is more likely to be one I will use to purchase a house. Sometimes the agent that does a dual job cannot concentrate on renting, so be careful.

HILDA'S HINT

Stay away from realtors who only think of their commissions. They will not last a long time in the marketplace.

A realtor is usually a very good judge of character. He or she should know if the tenants could potentially cause a problem. They have experience in dealing with the public, and a special ability to spot a disastrous tenant!

Have a good relationship with your realtor. When a realtor rents a house and the tenants want to return, whether it is a summer group, students or military personnel, I call the same realtor to re-rent the house. I could just rent it myself and save on the agent's commission, and I do not. That realtor thinks of me when they have prospective tenants.

If you have repeat tenants, the realtor should give you a discount on the commission, since they only have to re-process the paperwork.

Screening Tenants

After you or your realtor has made appointments to meet prospective tenants at the rental office or house, how do you decide who is a suitable tenant and who is not? You have already pre-screened people from your telephone conversations, and have agreed to meet with them to show the house. Aside from being a realtor or landlord, you are now also a salesperson. You need to "sell" the house and property, and convince the tenants that they will enjoy living in the house.

HILDA'S HINT

Treat your applicants as you would like to be treated if you were being interviewed as a tenant.

You should dress neatly, and be honest about the condition of the house. I like to make sure that the house is in good shape before showing tenants. If you are in the midst of upgrading or having some repairs done, advise the realtor or tenant of the status and the completion timeframe. You, as the landlord, have a right to decide whom you choose to live in your house.

Remember there are Federal, state and local guidelines on discrimination and other Fair Housing Rules that must be followed. You have the right to decline to rent to smokers or people with pets, and that must be stated in your lease. These issues should have already been addressed in your pre-screening telephone conversation.

The Federal Fair Housing Act prohibits discrimination on the basis of color, race, sex, religion, nationality, disability or familial status. This rule applies to all residential properties with a few exceptions. If you own a multiple dwelling unit and you live in one of the units, this federal law does not cover the other units. If you do not use a real estate agent to assist you in finding renters for your house, in other words if the house is offered for rent by the owner, discrimination is allowed. If the situation arises, you should check with your state and local guidelines or check with your real estate agent. The bottom line is, be fair to when deciding on a tenant.

Pets

Because all of my houses are furnished, I do not accept tenants with pets. You will get a broader range of applicants if you do accept pets. If a prospective tenant inquires, ask them questions about the pet. You may want to stay away from puppies that are not potty-trained, or unspayed cats, as they tend to make a mess in the house. If you have an appointment with a tenant with a pet, have them bring the pet to the house, on a leash, of course, for you to also "interview." Sometimes a little old lady, who has a cute middle-aged beagle for companionship, will be your best long-term tenant.

Tenant Application

After your walk-through of the house with your prospective tenant, give them a tenant application to complete. This is similar to a simple job application, to give you an idea of current living arrangements, job status and the like. If you are working with a real estate agent, they usually have their own standard application. In a situation where your real estate agent is screening the tenants, they will first have the tenant complete a pre-application, asking questions to make a determination of what types of houses they are interested in. In our area of Newport, the realtor also gives the tenant information on the Newport provision on noise and over-crowding. If one of my houses is chosen, the realtor calls me to negotiate the rent and utilities, or if there will be a cap on the utilities.

Sample Tenant Application Questions and Information

1. Have you previously rented in this area?

2. Do you know the rules and regulations imposed by Newport City Hall?

3. If you feel that you cannot follow City Hall Rules and my rules, I decline to rent to you.

4. A security deposit is required. For summer renters, the deposit will be slightly higher due to the increased risks.

5. Excessive noise and overcrowding in the house are not acceptable. There is a city fine of $500 in Newport for each lessee on the lease, per violation per day.

6. Garbage is required to be in a bag and the barrels placed at the curb on collection day. The city will impose a fine if these rules are not followed.

I have my real estate agents give more information and requirements to college students prior to having them sign a lease. Here are a few examples.

Rules for College Students:

1. Loud partying is not acceptable. We have neighbors to consider.

2. No frequent overnight guest visits. This causes problems in the neighborhood, and excessive traffic and parking problems. We have a nice neighborhood, we want to keep it that way!

3. If you have a party with liquor, and people become uncontrollable, neighbors will call the police because of the disturbance. I do not like middle- of-the-night phone calls informing me of these problems.

4. The house must be kept clean. My maintenance personnel or I will inspect the house periodically. If I am informed that the house looks more like a garbage dump than a house, I will not be happy. Excess garbage and mess attracts mice and other rodents.

5. Please do not remove the artwork from the walls of the house. When I am showing the house to prospective summer renters, I want it to be in the same condition as they will see it in the summer.

6. Your parents are required to send the rent before or on the first day of the month. I charge a late fee of $25.

7. If you remove the curtains because you do not like them, please put them back when you leave or you will be charged a penalty.

HILDA'S HINT

Be up front with prospective tenants. Lay down the ground rules so there will not be any confusion!

Credit Check

Do check your chosen applicants' credit, including their past employment history, renting history, and any large outstanding debt. There is often insufficient information given for you to make a good determination of the applicants. I rent to students and young families that do not always have a credit history. It is sometimes best to conduct your own search. You can call the person's employer and their current landlord to check the accuracy of their information and their rental history. Again, these should not be the only factors in making your decision, but it will help.

If you would like to do a professional credit check, you can contact a credit bureau that will handle your application for a small fee.

Here is an example of a professional credit check company:

Tenants Credit Report: 1-800-999-5603

$9.95 for a single report

$14.95 for a married couple

HILDA'S HINT

You should decide if this is cost-efficient for you. This service is not cheap, and may not always give you accurate information. You may also have to wait a few weeks for your answer. Remember time is money!

Leases

Your tenant has been screened, selected, checked and anxious to move in to the house! The last step prior to move-in is to have the tenant sign a lease agreement. The main purpose of the lease is to define the tenant and the landlord's obligations to each other and to the house. You may also want to have the tenant sign

HILDA'S HINT

A separate rental agreement is more effective, as the tenant usually does not read each and every word in the lease. If rules are spelled out in outline form on a rental agreement, tenants will tend to remember their responsibilities, and have a separate page for reference. Have them sign it!

a rental agreement. In Newport, the lease and rental agreements are combined so that nothing is overlooked. Check with your City Hall for the information in your town. As previously mentioned, the lease defines obligations while the rental agreement is a supplement defining responsibilities and "house rules." For example, the lease outlines the terms, length of stay, rental amount, utilities and security deposit, and more. The rental agreement describes lawn maintenance, appliance use, storage, furniture care and the like. You may choose to include the rental agreement information in your standard lease. If you have houses in different localities with different rules, you will have separate pieces of paper.

Security Deposit

In every lease ask for a security deposit. The amount may vary from one full month's rent, to first and last month's rent, or a month and a half rent. When I rent to summer vacationers, I usually ask for a security deposit of $2000. The reason for this is that summertime renters usually pose more of a risk. In Newport, we have strict City Hall rules and regulations. We have many visitors during the summer, and the town imposes strict noise abatement and other guidelines that they expect everyone to follow. I always return the security deposit within twenty days after the end of the lease.

There are many reasons why a landlord does not return the entire security deposit to the tenants. Here are a few:

- If there is a cap on the utility use, I multiply the number of months the tenants were in the house times the cap. That is their allowance during their stay. If they exceed the cap, I charge them the difference.

- If the house is left filthy, I charge a cleaning fee.

- If the tenants have removed pictures from the walls or have damaged the walls, I charge a fee.

- If there are boxes and junk left in the basement or garage, I charge a removal fee.

If the tenants have hired a cleaning person for their duration of the lease, I usually will not charge them a fee, even if the place has been left in disarray. After all, they have kept their end of the lease, and kept my house looking nice.

HILDA'S HINT

When returning the security deposit, send the check Priority Mail with delivery confirmation. This way, you are sure they receive it

I request the forwarding mailing address and e-mail address of each tenant, in order to reimburse each of them the security deposit. If a fee needs to be charged and the tenant is lacking money, I request that they reimburse me. Believe it or not, many of them have, and I thank them.

Rents

Should rent be due at the first of every month? Should tenants mail rent, pay cash or have you, as the landlord, pick it up at the house? Should a late fee be charged for past due rent? How often and how much should rent be increased? These are a few of the basic questions, which you will need to answer.

Due Date

Rent is due and should be paid in full by the first day of each month. Now remember, you have already collected the security deposit at the time the lease was signed. I do not tolerate late payments and charge a $25 per late fee. I also have the County Clerk send an eviction notice if necessary. This seldom happens, as I try to build a good relationship with my renters, especially the parents of my college student tenants.

Since I rent to various types of tenants, summer vacationers, military personnel and college students, as well as families, I impose different types of requirements for collecting the security deposit and rents. You can adapt my suggestions to your tenants as well.

Summer Rental

Between the month of December and the second week of April of the following year, all of the summer rents and the security deposits must be paid with installments. I usually rely on the realtor to handle this for me. Sometimes, the agent forgets to collect the security deposit before turning over possession of the house. Now I require the security deposit to be paid up front. It is important that I keep on top of this, as it is very difficult to get new tenants if the renters should default. All of the most desirable tenants will have already contracted their houses, and it may be too late. Summer tenants send their rents to the realtor, after paying the security deposit installments. The checks are then forwarded to me.

Military Personnel

Men and women in the military who rent my houses are usually very courteous and responsible. As soon as the officers decide to rent a house, they secure it with one-month rent and a security deposit. I usually have no trouble renting to the Navy. They send in their rents by mail, and usually pay very promptly.

I am very proud that I rent to men and women in the United States Navy. They get a bonus when they rent from me. If their ship docks in Manila in the Philippines, I rent a van for them to tour the historical sites, visit the shops and the suburbs. If I happen to be in Manila, I am the tour guide; if not, my sister does the honors.

College Students

When college students are in their sophomore year, they usually start to look for a place to live in September, for the following year when they will be juniors. I require them to pay the first month rent upon signing the lease, and they can pay me their security deposit by March or April prior to summer break. I also require that all parents send the rent before or on the first day of each month. When the student pays me the rent directly, they tend to be late or have insufficient funds in the bank. I have learned my lesson and now have the parents mail it to me.

HILDA'S HINT

Keep your rental rate comparable to other houses in the neighborhoods. It is difficult to rent your house if your rent is much higher than the other houses.

I think everyone should be required to mail the rent. It saves the tenant as well as the landlord valuable time. The tenants will usually mail their checks together in one envelope, representing the address for each house. As mentioned earlier, the college students' parents mail their rent monthly. I log each check as it is delivered with the amount and the date. We will cover my accounting system in a future chapter.

Each December, I go to the real estate offices to update the rents and security deposits. I play it by ear when deciding if I increase the rental amount, or not. Again, it depends on the going rate in the neighborhoods. The best source for this information is the real estate agent.

Calendar for Maintenance

I prepare a calendar each October for the upcoming year, and distribute it to my maintenance personnel and to the realtors in late December. Most prospective tenants will call as early as December to reserve their summer rental for the next year.

Repeat summer tenants reserve their place for the next year, as soon as they arrive on their vacation on Memorial Weekend.

By the end of March, the cleaning groups will know their dates of work. If they have to clean three houses in one day, they know when they need help. I use a pink highlighter pen to indicate specific days on the calendar.

The vacancies in the calendar (the unmarked dates) are the days to do inside repairs such as painting, caulking bathrooms and other repairs. The days marked with an "X" denotes the property is occupied.

I keep one calendar for each property and have included a sample in the back of this book.

CHAPTER 6 Accounting

Hands-on is the name of the game! I need to know the ins and outs of cash flow, whether it is positive or negative. This is how you learn to run the business and maintain control over cash flow.

My husband works full-time, and property management is my sideline. The benefits from real estate taxes help us immensely in our tax planning and future planning. Timing is very important in the world of tax planning. One way that your tax return can be affected by the timing of paying expenses is called the Cash Method. This means that your income is taxed and your expenses are deducted in the same year that the expenses are paid and the income is received. In other words the money you earn from rent, and the money you pay for expenses pertaining to the rental property in the year 2002, can be included in your tax return for the same year.

HILDA'S HINT

Use the Cash Method, it is easier to prepare the bookkeeping and easier on your accountant!

An alternative to the Cash Method is the Accrual Method. Using this method you will need to account for the rent received (income) as it is paid to you, and deduct the expenses as they incur. Accountants may also refer to the Accrual Method as "Earned Income", which means it is applied to the current month, not totaled for the year. This method can be very confusing, especially if you own more than one property. If rents are late, or if you are spending money on renovations or repairs on an empty property, this method will not be accurate. The Accrual Method is mainly used by large businesses or corporations.

Paying Bills

When I started to buy houses, the bank account for our rental properties was mixed in with our personal checking account. I taught my husband the system for paying our personal house bills similar to the way I had taught him to pay his office bills. The accounting became more complicated as I bought more houses. It was also getting very confusing. My husband was now complaining that he was paying all the bills of the houses, but completely ignored the fact that he receives rent for these houses!

HILDA'S HINT

Most of us pay our own personal bills. Why should you hire a bookkeeper to pay your business bills? Remember...hands-on!!

To solve this problem, I separated the houses into six accounts. I put one to two houses in each account, which were opened at my brokerage firm. I chose this firm because they pay higher yield on your cash compared to the banks. They also give me personal attention. It is more manageable to handle the cash flow, negative or positive, of all of the houses. I balance each account every month.

As I receive the invoices and statements, I put them in a container and clip them together according to house number. The bills are paid three times a month. Every ten days I enter the information into the computer. As mentioned previously, my husband is in charge of paying the bills for the condo in South Carolina, the time-share property, our house bills and his office bills.

HILDA'S HINT

Obtain a business credit card that will give you airline miles for each purchase you make. You will not believe how much mileage it will give you. Why not earn a free trip while spending money on your rental houses?

It is difficult to pay bills every day or every few days. As the invoices are received, check the items listed to be sure that you really ordered or purchased the item or service. If there is any discrepancy, call the company immediately to straighten it out. After a statement is paid, I insert it into a manila envelope marked with each house number.

Try to open a credit line at different stores so that you are only invoiced once a month. If you are placing orders more than twice a month, it is easier to only receive one billing statement. This will save you time, paperwork and hassle!

I usually use only one credit card for purchasing items from my suppliers, so it will not be confused with personal items that I charge. I always use a separate credit card for personal purchases. Immediately after purchasing an item in the store, I write the house number on the front of the receipt.

Holding Ownership of Your Property

There are different ways to hold your properties:

1. Sole proprietorship
2. Corporation
3. Partnership
4. Limited Liability Company
5. Trust

1. **Sole Proprietorship**: This simply means that you hold the property in your name or in your name and your spouse's name. Your income taxes are very simple and you can put all of your assets in your will. On the other hand, your personal name will be listed on all of your records and your assets can be easily targeted in a lawsuit.

2. **Corporation**: According to law, a 'corporation' is a person whose complete assets, property and businesses are now under a corporate name, not your personal name. Some people choose to form a corporation to impress and act more professional. I guess it is the only way that most of us will ever be able to be called "President!"

   Corporations can limit your liability. In other words if a corporation is involved in a lawsuit, your personal assets cannot be touched. Obviously, if you are sued personally and do not have a corporation you could stand to lose everything you have worked so hard to achieve. There is more paperwork and "red tape" involved with a corporation.

   The property is not listed in your personal name, and you may be able to receive more tax advantages as opposed to being a sole proprietorship. You can also have investors in a corporation. If you need to raise capital for purchasing more properties, you can sell a portion of the other properties to your investors.

3. **Partnership:** This is defined as when two or more people enter into a written agreement, and each partner is involved jointly in the decision-making. I do not recommend a partnership, as there are too many complications. Remember that old saying, "Never lend money to a friend"? Well, you should never enter into business with a friend if you want to remain friends; there always seems to be problems.

4. **Limited Liability Company:** This is how I hold my properties. The LLC offers the same protection as a corporation but you have more flexibility, especially with tax advantages. It also utilizes the advantages of partnerships but it limits your personal liability. My attorney and accountants have advised me that this is the best way to go when owning real estate.

   It is acceptable to have a one-person LLC, but each state varies with their rules and regulations, since this is a new type of corporation. You have the choice of deciding how you would like to be taxed. It can be as an individual, a partnership, or a corporation. Your accountants will advise you on what is best in your situation.

5. **Trust:** Holding your property in trust is a popular way to hold your properties. There are three basic types of trusts: living trust, revocable trust, and irrevocable trusts. The basic definitions are: a Living Trust is normally used as an alternative to a will; a Revocable Trust is one that can be revised at any time, an Irrevocable Trust cannot have any changes or addendums.

   By creating a trust, you are entrusting another person or attorney with your properties. The manager of the trust is called a "trustee". The trustee's job is to handle the legalities for the beneficiary of the trust, which most of the time would be you, the property owner. The beneficiary lets the trustee know what he or she wants done with the properties, and the trustee carries out the wishes or actions. The trustee can also advise what he or she feels is in the best interest of the beneficiary.

   I just recently moved our trust to another attorney, John Harpootian, who had advised me to have members of my family as trustees. I am my husband's trustee, and vice-versa. When we are both gone, our son will take over. Look for a good estate attorney. He or she will give you all of your different options.

HILDA'S HINT

Make a list to weigh the pros and cons of the different ways of protecting your property. Ask the advice of your attorney and accountant to see which would best work for you.

Accountants

When I started buying houses I did everything by hand when preparing the books for the accountant, and I was very systematic. I asked an acquaintance who happened to be a graduate of computer science, to order and set up a computer for me. She could not handle teaching me, because I had no computer knowledge.

I asked my friends for referrals to accountants. I interviewed a few of them until I felt at ease with one.

I called an accounting firm in search of an accountant. One of my doctor friends recommended him. I called him in the morning and he asked me when I would be available to meet with him. Of course, I said…now. He was there when I arrived. I had brought two years of income tax returns from my husband's office and our personal tax information. I asked about his fees

The accountant assigned to our accounts was instructed on our situation. The first person assigned to me had left and Brian Frenette assumed the duties of teaching me computer skills. Brian is very smart and extremely patient. He set up a new program compatible to their office's program on my computer. He comes to my house once a month to give me instructions. When he comes back, I am supposed to have that lesson from the previous month mastered. He will then give me another lesson on another aspect of accounting. After six months, I became good at it. Now Brian comes every three to five months to retrieve the information that I put in, or as needed to assist in more complicated transactions. By the end of the year, we were done and it was easy for them to do our tax returns. I also saved a lot of money by keeping the books and records myself. It is good also for their office because they do not need to hire another person to handle my accounts.

HILDA'S HINT

I learned to balance the statements every month and I am conscious of the mistakes because I am handling our bookkeeping. I can have a better handle on the funds and know exactly where they have been allocated.

I submit the required paperwork to my accountant in the middle of January each year. I expect him to complete my tax returns early so that I will not have to pay any penalties or late fees. I will search for another accountant if my tax returns are overlooked or pushed to the wayside for someone else's. I am on time with my submissions therefore the accountant should complete my paperwork early as I request. I am very strict with them. Sometimes I feel that I am advising the accountant rather than them advising me. It is like a pineapple upside-down cake! When my taxes are not done early in the year, it restricts me from starting my strategic tax planning for the forthcoming year.

My computer instructor, Brian Frenette, wrote the following to give us an overview of the accounting principles of real estate.

Investing in Real Estate

Investing in real estate offers various economic opportunities. The main purpose is to maximize both financial and tax advantages. One must evaluate each real estate investment when deciding to acquire a property and continually during it's operations. Areas of importance revolve around the property's potential for cash flow and appreciation. Most rental properties generate a tax loss and may still maintain a positive cash flow. Many times the tax loss is attributable to depreciation. Therefore, if the income from rentals and tax loss (benefit) do not cover the cost of operating the property, this may not be a wise investment.

After acquiring a rental property, you must consider the various tax advantages and available devices. Some of the most advantageous devices or entities available are the C and S Corporation and the Limited Liability Company. Selecting the type of entity depends on issues stemming from the investor's particular tax situation.

Just when you thought you were finished, there are two forms of accounting used by small businesses—cash and accrual. You must select between the two and notify the IRS on your tax return. The main difference between the cash and accrual method is the timing of recording income and expenses. Choosing the best method can be determined by the nature of your business, it's legal structure and whether or not you extend credit.

Maintaining a successful operation should begin by establishing an internal control structure which will include a good bookkeeping system. Generating controls over operations starts with the questions, who? when? where? and how? Determining and sticking to a controlled process will ensure security and efficiency over operations.

An exceptional bookkeeping system begins with organization and preparation. Bookkeeping is basically recording income and expenses.

Whoever is entering the data should have a good understanding of the debit and credit double entry system as well as the different account types, which make up the end products of financial reporting.

As a cash basis taxpayer the checkbook transactions would be recorded to a manual ledger system or preferably to a computerized accounting software system. There are many accounting software programs. Ranging from high-end complex to low-end, user-friendly packages. If used correctly, good accounting software will do half of the bookkeeping work for you as well as increase efficiency. In selecting accounting software, here are a few items to consider: 1) User friendly in its functionality and appearance 2) Useable features 3) Ability to upgrade 4) Security and controls 5) Technical support 6) On-line capabilities 7) price. The end result of a good bookkeeping system will generate financial reports useful in making decisions, evaluating the investment and tax planning and preparation.

The topics discussed here should be further researched in depth and discussed with a professional due to the difference in everyone's particular situation.

Brian Frenette
Senior Accountant
Restivo Wisehart L.L.P.

Record Keeping

I believe that the best way to keep the most accurate records on your rental houses is with a computer. Now remember, computers should not scare you if you have never ventured into the world of Bill Gates! I had no knowledge of computer programs or record keeping and through patience and perseverance I can say now that I am computer literate! You can take classes at the local schools, hire a tutor, or buy a book. It will save you a lot of money by doing the simple tasks of record keeping yourself.

A friend of mine gave me the CD *Mavis Beacon Teaches Typing* for a Christmas gift one year. I inserted it into the computer and practiced faithfully. The better you can type, the faster you can work. I had never typed much, as I always paid someone to type my term papers and theses in school. Well, that was in the 1960s! It was time I learned to do it myself! That was one of the best gifts I ever received.

Basically you will need to keep track of two items. How much money comes in and how much money goes out. In other words, keep track of your income and expenses. As you become more experienced, you can also prepare information for your accountant; prepare forms, write newsletters, and prepare forms or signs for your tenants.

I thought my records were organized prior to putting them on the computer. Now I can save valuable time and money and there is less room for error. The computer can do it all!

Car Mileage Expense

This is one area that many landlords forget about when logging expenses. Car mileage is a deductible expense as long as the trips are directly related to your rental properties. You can create a mileage log on your computer and keep it on a clipboard in your car. This way you will never forget to log your mileage. You will need to include where you were driving to, why you went there, the amount of miles that you drove and the date and time. Train yourself from the start to log your mileage daily. You may want to print a calendar from you computer and attach it to your clipboard.

Try not to estimate your mileage. You will probably be traveling to the same stores, going from your personal residence to your rental properties and other similar trips. Many trips will have the same mileage. Once you set your odometer once to clock the miles, you will just have to log the date and time of your journey.

HILDA'S HINT

Add inputting your mileage log to your weekly computer tasks. Simply keeping the log written in pen will fade and the papers will get crinkled and possibly lost. The computer is the way to go!

Some examples of logging your car mileage would be:

- Driving to the bank to deposit your rent checks
- Driving to the hardware store to purchase supplies
- Driving to your rental house to show it to prospective tenants

I think you get the idea. It is very important not to say, "Oh, I will log the mileage later," because you will forget.

HILDA'S HINT

Keep all of your receipts no matter how big or small the purchase. Any amount of money that is spent on your property should be recorded.

Receipts

It is a good idea to set a time for yourself each week to log your receipts onto your computer, expenses for that week. Buy a small file box to deposit the receipts after shopping, and reconcile them weekly. You may want to write the store and item purchased on the front of the receipt, as some stores just list the item number and the subtotal and totals. Also remember you may be purchasing other personal items on that same store receipt. Circle the items pertaining to the rental properties for quick tallying. The computer can add the totals for you.

Keep your receipts separated according to store or vendor, until you get your monthly statement or credit card invoice. It is easier to look for a receipt when it is in its supplier envelope, rather than in a separate house envelope. Once you have checked the receipt off as listed on your statement, put it in your house envelope.

As receipts began to pile up when I first began buying the houses, I purchased a plastic container and labeled 10 x 13 manila envelopes, and placed them in the container. I put the house number on the envelope and filed them according to corporation name. As I paid each bill I placed it in the envelope. At the end of the year, I submit everything to the accountant along with the receipts.

The Internal Revenue Service is a stickler for asking for receipts should you ever get audited. Presenting the receipts is not enough, and it will be impossible for you to remember each and every item purchased.

Make sure to also ask each maintenance personnel, service technician and any other 'hired hand' to give you a receipt for their services. A cancelled check is not enough proof. It is acceptable to pay for services in cash. I always pay with a check, so I will have not only the company's receipt for services but also the cancelled check, and everything will match. Services that independent contractors provide over the amount of $600 require a 1099 form to be submitted into the IRS. These forms can be obtained through the IRS or your accountant.

HILDA'S HINT

Ask your accountant to prepare the 1099 and mail it to the contractors

I advise those who like to venture into the world of real estate to get a good accountant who specializes in real estate. At first we decided to do a sole proprietorship, but it was not tax advantageous to us when I acquired more houses. I decided to look for a better accountant who would be challenged with this problem. I also have a trust lawyer who complements the decision of the accountant. We will discuss attorneys in Chapter 8. We decided on forming a limited liability company (LLC), along with a trust. This way the accounting and taxes will be calculated as a partnership. With this decision, it got easier when reconciling the accounting for each house. I am no longer going insane with confusion over paying the bills!

Income Taxes

One of the first questions usually asked on the subject of income tax is, "What expenses can I deduct on my income taxes?" The answer to that question is very basic when it comes to real estate, but will require the expert knowledge of your accountant to complete. Most expenses that you incur while owning rental properties are legitimate business deductions.

Your accountant will give you up to date rules and regulations regarding the allowed deductions, which normally include interest, property taxes, insurance, utilities and basic operating expenses such as supplies, legal fees and landscaping.

Depreciation

The house itself is even a tax deduction. There are many rules and regulations enforced by the Internal Revenue Service. For example, you can write off a fraction of the home cost and appliances under what is called, "depreciation." A portion of the costs will be written off each year until the total cost is written off. Depreciation is important when you sell your rental property, particularly if you lose money in the transaction. Your accountant will have the latest regulations and updates on depreciation.

Home Office

The IRS allows certain home office deductions. Deducting portions of your home and utilities, and deducting a percentage of your primary residence being utilized as a business office are red flags, which could incur a tax audit. Particularly in your first year of owning rental property, be smart when taking deductions. Deducting extravagant dinners, your new Mercedes, and lavish shopping sprees probably will not hold up with the IRS!

Justifiable deductions are certainly office furniture, office supplies, a computer system, bookkeeping and accounting fees. My best advice would be to save your receipts, prepare them in an orderly manner and *Give Them to Your Accountant!* Leave this in the hands of the experts. There may also be items that you will be able to deduct on the advice of your accountant that never occurred to you!

Supplies

This is a fairly obvious income tax deduction. Any supply or item that you purchase for repair, replacement or inclusion in your rental property or its yard can be considered a business expense and is deductible on your income tax. I cannot stress the importance once again of saving every single receipt from your purchases. This will be needed should you get audited by the IRS, and will speed up your accountant's tax preparation at the end of the year.

House Renovations and Repairs

The rule of thumb is that repairs are generally tax-deductible for the year that they were completed. House renovations are generally amortized over a period of years. In other words, when you make a repair, deduct it immediately; and when you renovate a room, or the entire house, it will be depreciated.

HILDA'S HINT

Hire an accountant to help you with your income taxes; it will save you money, time and headaches in the long run!

Real Estate Taxes

Paying real estate taxes is mandatory by the Federal government. The bright side is, real taxes are tax deductible! The tax on your property is based on the assessed value, based on the market value on similar properties. Tax assessors will tend to set the assessed value slightly lower than the true market value. You will need to be sure that the appraised property value does not exceed the market value.

Let us simplify that last statement… market value is the price you can get for your property if you sell it. There are many factors that comprise market value:

- A house will have a different market value in the summer than the winter.
- A house with a finished basement will have a higher market value.
- A house with a fireplace, deck or porch will have a higher market value.

HILDA'S HINT

Sometimes you need to spend money to enhance the value of your house. Special added improvements will attract sellers, and they could be "deal-makers" when sellers are looking at similar houses.

The more added 'extras" you have in your house, the higher the selling price or market value.

A few times per year, I ask a realtor to give me a market analysis of my houses to check for their appreciation. This is very important in the strategy of my business.

CHAPTER 7 Attorneys, Insurance, and Tenant Problems

Do You Need an Attorney?

The answer to that question is most definitely, yes! Most states require that an attorney handle the legal paperwork for the title insurance, mortgage and other details of real estate transactions. In some states, such as California, an attorney is not needed because the realtor and the escrow company handle all of the legal paperwork.

The main task of the real estate attorney is to run a title search to be sure that the title is clear prior to purchasing the property. In other words, he or she will check to see that there are no outstanding liens or debts on the property. The title search will inform the attorney about the chain of the title, who owns it, and what, if any liens exist. It will also show if there is a mortgage, the amount of property tax, and if there are any judgments against the property. If there are debts or liens against the house, the title insurance investigator will try to relieve them before issuing a title insurance policy. If these liens cannot be resolved, I do not purchase the property.

HILDA'S HINT

Find an attorney who can help you, as the landlord, on other issues aside from the closing of the property. You will get to know him, and he can assist you in all tasks from simple tenant violations to eviction.

I tend to use an attorney who is involved with my mortgage company. He or she is protecting the lender, so he might as well protect me too! The process seems to go much smoother when there is only one attorney involved. There is no bickering back and forth between attorneys, and the paperwork seems to flow and is finished much faster.

Liability, Property and Casualty Insurance

All houses must be protected with insurance. I have dealt with the same insurance company for more than twenty-five years and I have a wonderful relationship with the Assistant vice-president. She always researches the best rates and insurance companies that will best suit each property.

I make certain that replacement value and extended insurance are enforced. Full replacement value is especially important when receiving reimbursement for submitted claims. If you do not have full replacement value, you will receive payment only for the depreciated value of your loss. For example, if your stove was considered a loss due to a fire, if you have full replacement value you would receive payment on the claim for the full cost of a new comparable item at the current cost. If you did not have full replacement value, you receive a portion of what the oven is worth today. If the oven was twenty years old, well, you can figure out the math.

You also need to update the insurance value if your house appraisal has increased. This is very important! If you add anything to the house that increases the value, for example, a deck or a renovation, and you have a new appraisal, you must notify your insurance agent.

I keep an insurance chart to be sure that all of the houses have sufficient coverage.

In order to help us all better understand the various terms and definitions in the insurance world, I have asked one of my insurance brokers, Donald J. Curran, to give us some further information, which you will find at the end of this chapter.

Hazard Insurance

In order to get mortgage approval, you will need to purchase Hazard Insurance. This is also sometimes called Homeowner's Insurance or Fire Insurance. The lender will require you to have sufficient coverage, because a major loss such as a fire is more of a risk to them than to you. You can shop around for the best rates for your Hazard policy. Begin with obtaining an estimate from your current insurance broker. Even if you only have car insurance policies with a certain company, they will often give you a discount for a multiple line policy. In other words, the more policies in different areas that you have with the company, the better rate you will receive.

There are many types of Hazard Insurance, which your agent will discuss with you. You can obtain the basic coverage that is required by your lender, which will cover eleven basic perils or types of problems. The following is a list of the basic coverages:

- Lightning or fire
- Loss of property from the premises due to fire or other peril
- Hail or windstorm
- Explosion
- Riot and civil uprising
- Aircraft
- Vehicle
- Smoke
- Vandalism
- Theft
- Breakage of glass which constitutes a part of the structure

You can purchase extended coverage or a Broad Insurance Policy. This type of policy will include the perils named in the above basic coverage along with the following:

- Falling objects
- Weight of ice, snow or sleet

- Collapsing of the building or part of the building
- Sudden tearing, cracking, burning or bulging of a steam or hot water heating system or other appliance
- Freezing of plumbing, heating, air-conditioning or other appliance
- Sudden or accidental injury from generated current to electrical appliance, fixture or wiring

HILDA'S HINT

Discuss all possible insurance options with your agent. Obtain at least two or three estimates for coverage costs. As insurance is basically the same across the board, base your decision on customer service, optional coverage and rates.

These are the two basic coverages. Again, your insurance agent again will advise you if additional coverage is necessary for the particular type of house you are purchasing. For example if you live in a warm climate where there is no threat of snow or ice, and you are purchasing a fairly new house with up to date electrical wiring and appliances, you may not need the extended coverage.

Renter's Insurance

I include an addendum in all of my tenants' leases that it is recommended for them to obtain their own Renter's Insurance. The basic annual cost is a few hundred dollars, and the insurance protects the tenant's personal property in the house. Renter's Insurance does not cover loss or damage to the building structure in any way. It is solely to protect the tenant's personal belongings.

HILDA'S HINT

Have the tenant provide a copy of their insurance policy to you prior to signing the lease. This will provide unnecessary problems in the future, should there be any insurance claims filed.

For example, if the electrical wiring starts a fire in the house and the house burns down, the tenant has lost all or most of his personal property. Hazard insurance does not cover the tenants' personal items, and will not replace them. On a rental house, there is no need for me to take purchase All-Risk Insurance coverage, which most people obtain on their primary residence. (This includes Basic Insurance, Broad Insurance and personal property losses.) As a landlord, I am not responsible for tenants' personal property; therefore, I do not pay to insure it.

If the tenant does not want to take Renter's Insurance, you may want to think twice about renting your property to them.

Worker's Compensation Insurance

This insurance is commonly overlooked. Everyone who works on your property should hold Worker's Compensation Insurance. All contractors and subcontractors, whether they are landscapers, electricians or plumbers, need to have this coverage for their employees.

For example, if a plumber worked on the pipes in your house, slipped and fell on the water and broke his neck, you would be responsible for these injuries if he did not possess Worker's Compensation Insurance. Would your insurance policy cover this claim? Do you really want to find out the answer to that question? I certainly would not. Ask each service technician for a copy of his or her worker's compensation policy. If they do not hold one, do not take the chance. There are many other contractors who would be happy to present you with a copy of their policy.

You can check with your attorney or City Hall for specific rules and regulations in your city and state regarding subcontractors. Each state varies, but if you have a technician sign a subcontractor agreement, they are generally responsible for their own actions as well as insurance.

If you employ these technicians directly, then you are responsible for providing them with Worker's Compensation Insurance. This is something that you do not need to get involved with, and should hire only personnel who can provide you with a copy of their policy.

City Hall Regulations

Check with your local City Hall about specific rules and regulations for all residents. Since tenants are residents, this means that your tenants must also abide by local rules. City Hall has a "no tolerance" policy when it comes to violations. The rules are imposed to help keep Newport a safe and desirable city for its residents. If your city does not have guidelines, you can adapt these if applicable:

A Partial Summary Adapted from The City of Newport, Rhode Island, Ordinance from City Hall

The city requires notice to be placed within view of the rental dwelling unit, which constitutes compliance.

Trash Collection and Recycling
Sanitary Services Corporation perform trash and recycling collections. Trash and recyclable objects are collected once a week at curbside. All material to be collected must be placed at curbside by 6a.m. The following items are included in the mandatory-recycling program:

- Aluminum and tin cans
- Glass bottles and jars
- #1 and #2 plastics
- Newspapers, magazines, office paper
- Cardboard flattened and bundled

Dwelling Occupancy Limits
The Newport Zoning Ordinance limits the number of unrelated individuals who may reside in the dwelling unit to five. Any number of unrelated individuals greater than five constitutes an ordinance violation under the jurisdiction of the Newport Municipal Court and a possible fine of up to $500.00.

Residential Parking Program
The City of Newport requires sticker parking on certain city streets during the months of May through October. A one-year residential parking permit can be purchased for $2.00. Violations of this program will result in fines.

Noise
It is a policy of the City of Newport to promote an environment free from excessive noise that degrades the quality of life of the city and its residents. A noise disturbance consists of any sound, which exceeds acceptable decibel levels.

Should the police be summoned to calm a disturbance, an additional summons will be issued in addition to the initial noise disturbance summons.

Tenant Problems

If a problem arises and a tenant does not adhere to the regulations you must act fast!

Call your realtor to help mediate the problem

Visit the tenants early in the morning. Discuss with them the pros and cons of the consequences, and have your lawyer contact them.

Contact your lawyer, and discuss the issues with him or her

Prepare for quick eviction if necessary

There are ways to avoid tenant problems, although this is not always foolproof! Prior to signing the lease, discuss the city's ordinances and your own rules with them. Include a section in your lease which advises them of the consequences should they break one of the rules. Have them initial this section to be sure that they understand. My realtors warn prospective tenants time and time again prior to finalizing the lease.

If you own a condominium or a townhouse, chances are the association will have a clause written into their bylaws, which the tenant needs to read and understand prior to signing. Many associations also hire some type of security guard to wander around the premises looking for violations, stopping tenants before they get carried away!

Tenant Complaints

You should always assume that your tenants are nice, honest people unless they give you just cause to believe otherwise! Most tenants feel that their landlord is at their beck and call day or night. You need to train them from the day they move in, that all problems and annoyances with appliances, the yard and even neighbors are not always emergencies. If a water pipe bursts and there is water pouring into the basement of the house, that is a true emergency and they should immediately contact you as the landlord and owner of the house, or your designated maintenance personnel.

A tenant pays good money for a nice house to live in, and problems should be addressed as soon as possible. Leaving a list of helpful hints may deter a middle of the night phone call for help. For example, most of my tenants work or attend school and do their laundry at night. If the washer or dryer fails to work properly, the tenants have instructions from me to call the repair company directly and leave a message with the problem. If it is too costly to repair, I will usually purchase a new model. I also instruct my tenants that if they have no heat or water, they should call the respective company directly. We pay for service contracts and the repair person will arrive immediately to remedy the problem.

HILDA'S HINT

Leave a list of examples of what is an emergency and what is not. A leak in the roof during the winter *is* an emergency and should merit an immediate phone call to you. A garage door opener that does not work is *not* an emergency. The opener always has a manual switch; it can wait until the next day to be repaired

You do not necessarily want your tenant to make any repairs to your house. After all, you have your qualified maintenance team to handle the repairs. If a tenant is making constant phone calls to you with problems, you may want to think twice about renewing their next lease. Some people are definitely more trouble than they are worth!

Tenant Requests

Included in the lease agreement is information on utility payments (whether they are included in the rent or not), and information on what appliances come with the house.

HILDA'S HINT

If the client is adamant about a change in the house, offer to split it with them 50/50. This may change their mind completely, or they may agree. Then, you have added the value to your house for only half of the cost!

During the course of the lease, if a tenant requests something not mentioned in the lease, you are not always required to provide the item as a convenience. Remember that the tenant is aware of what is in the house prior to moving in, and prior to signing the lease. If there is a claw foot bathtub without a shower in one of the house's bathrooms, you should not have to convert it to a shower just because the tenant is requesting it. It would certainly add value to your house, but at this time you may not have the extra money to fund the change. You want your tenants to be satisfied and like living in your house, but it should not be a "money pit" for you to keep spending money.

"Bad" Checks

It is the tenant's responsibility to pay you the monthly rent on time and with sufficient funds in their bank account. If a tenant has been paying on time each month, and you have not had a problem cashing their check, you are lucky. Problems can happen even to the best tenants. They may change their bank and the account may show insufficient funds causing their rent check to bounce! Ask the bank to redeposit the check and contact the tenant to inform them of the situation, and most tenants will rectify the situation immediately. When there are those tenants who may truly not have the funds in their bank account to pay you for the rent, what do you do? How do you handle this? Do you need to evict them?

In the state of Rhode Island there are strict eviction laws, and there is also my "no tolerance" policy. If you do not pay me the rent, I cannot pay the mortgage and I will get charged a late fee. I can find someone else to live in the house who will pay the rent. No one likes to go through an eviction, but there are times when this is your only option. Contact your attorney to walk you through it. If you have a signed lease agreement that is the first step in the right direction to win your case. Failure to pay rent is cause for eviction. No, you cannot throw the people out on the street, or change the locks on the house while they are at work, but you can file papers with the city and start the eviction process.

You should first try to work out the situation with the tenant. Do not just run to City Hall with the lease agreement in one hand and the bounced check in the other. There may be a valid reason why the check bounced, and if you do not ask you will never find out.

A bad check is a serious offense. If the check is re-deposited and it clears, you have every right as the landlord to ask the tenant for reimbursement of the bank fees. In fact, this should be included as a clause in the lease agreement to avoid confusion.

During all these years, I received one check that 'bounced.' I called the tenant several times and he completely ignored the call, so I filed a claim in small claims court. The tenant even ignored the court! As the tenant now lives in Massachusetts, I let my attorney handle it from here.

Eviction

You should check with your state and/or your attorney for the specific rules of eviction. Here are a few basic steps that you must follow to evict a tenant:

Send a registered letter to the tenant (because they have to sign for it) giving them formal notice that you are evicting them.

File an "Action for Eviction" at your county's small claims court division. The court will schedule a date for the court hearing, and they will ask how you want the notice served to the defendant (the tenant.)

You must serve, or have the county serve, the defendant with the official eviction notice. It is better to have a third-party person serving the notice, do not involve yourself in this. You have enough to deal with.

> **HILDA'S HINT**
>
> 
>
> **Remember that having a bad tenant is far worse than having no tenant at all! The house is better being empty for a month, rather than having it destroyed or neglected by a bad tenant.**

You must appear in court on the day of the hearing. In small claims court you will most likely be representing yourself. State the facts, bring in your information, you have the law on your side in this case.

Upon your victory, the court will demand that the tenant pay you all past due rents including late fees. You may also opt to use the tenant's security deposit to recoup part of the payments.

As I mentioned before, no one wants to go through an eviction. Try to resolve your problems before this step unless it is inevitable.

Insurance Definitions

"Here are some insurance definitions. Insurance is a vast industry and the definitions are from a primary insurance source. After thirty years, it has been a very interesting, educational and rewarding business. It is complex and very much tied into contract law."

Donald J. Curran, CIC, Senior Vice-President
Starkweather & Shepley Insurance Brokerage, Inc.

Risk: Chance of a loss; uncertainty of loss; probability that a loss will occur.

Loss: An incident, which results in financial loss

- Direct Loss: actual destruction to insured property (dwelling fire)
- Indirect Loss: another form of financial loss resulting from the Direct Loss (loss of rents)

Property: Any tangible property; tangible assets

Liability: A negligent act, which causes injury to another person (Bodily Injury) or damage to property belonging to another (Property Damage).

Negligence: The failure to act in a reasonable or prudent manner (generally the result of carelessness, ignorance, thoughtlessness or inaction, all non-intentional).

Peril/Cause of Loss: The specific event that caused the loss (fire, lightning, flood, etc.)

Named Peril Coverage: Each of the covered perils is specifically named in the policy.

Open Perils Coverage: The policy does not list named perils but states that it will pay for any peril except for those specifically excluded in the policy.

Indemnify: To restore an insured, who suffers a loss, to his original financial condition prior to the loss.

Claim Settlement Options:

- ACTUAL CASH VALUE: Replacement Cost less depreciation
- REPLACEMENT COST: To repair or replace with like kind or quality (without deduction for depreciation), subject to the Limit of Liability shown on the policy.
- EXTENDED REPLACEMENT COST: To repair or replace with like kind or quality, not subject to the Limit of Liability on the insurance policy.

Exclusions: Losses which the policy specifically states are not covered by the insurance contract. Examples:

- CATASTROPHIC LOSSES: such as war, nuclear catastrophes, flood and earthquake.
- LOSSES BETTER COVERED ELSEWHERE: Homeowners policies exclude Auto Losses, which are better covered under an Automobile policy.
- PREDICTABLE LOSSES: such as deterioration, wear and tear, rust and mechanical breakdown, which does NOT result from a fortuitous event.

Coinsurance Clause: An insurance condition that rewards insureds who purchase adequate levels of insurance and penalizes those insureds who do not.

Limit of Liability: The maximum that can be collected under the policy for any one loss.

Vacancy/Unoccupancy: Unoccupancy means that no people are there. Vacancy means there are no people and no furniture, fixtures or equipment in the insured location.

Endorsement: A written modification to a policy (either an addition, deletion or change in the policy).

Accident: A sudden, unforeseen and unintended (fortuitous) event that happens at a known place and at a known time.

Occurrence: An accident including continuous and repeated exposure to injurious conditions, which result in bodily injury or property damage.

Some definitions taken from *Property & Casualty Pathfinder, Seventh Edition,* Pathfinder Publishers, Indianapolis IN (www.4insuranceEd.com)

CHAPTER 8 Hilda's Strategy

When my friends learned that I managed houses, they said to me, "What is your secret?" or "What is your formula?" They are always trying to figure out if real estate is a good investment and will give them a good return on their money. I tell my friends, "I do not have a formula." I also tell them that it all depends on the strategy, and how hard you are willing to work. You need to have foresight. If you work hard, the money will cover most or all of your expenses, and will even give you a little bit extra! You can invest that extra money in mutual funds to give you security for a household emergency, like when you need a new roof!

I do not spend hours each month calculating the return on my investment. If I did, I would probably go insane. I leave this job to my accountant. He gives me the figures at the end of tax season.

Develop a Plan and Set Your Goals

It is a good idea when in business to put together a plan, whether it is short-term or long-term, and set goals for yourself on what you would like to accomplish. Do not set goals so high that they are out of reach, because then you will be disappointed with yourself. Do set goals that you feel you can achieve, and remember that old saying, "Rome was not built in a day!" You will not become a millionaire in real estate overnight, although you can make a comfortable living and a lot of extra pocket money!

Ask yourself a few questions:

- Do you have the patience to buy a fixer-upper house and complete the renovations?

- Do you want to buy houses and immediately turn them around to sell for a profit?

- Do you want to buy houses which need little work, maybe just cosmetic "sprucing up," and have tenants to pay your mortgage?

Whichever avenue you take be happy with yourself and have patience. I choose the last scenario. I do not mind doing small renovations and repairs to the houses. After all no house is perfect. Even new houses will always need something done, such as landscaping, painting or wallpapering. I chose to buy houses, make them more attractive to perspective tenants, and collect rent. I am a "people person" and enjoy working with others and meeting people from all walks of life.

Investing in real estate is a long-term commitment. You should set your goals for about four or five years in the future. How many houses do you want to have in five years? Do you want to expand to condominiums, time-shares or apartment buildings? Do you want to eventually own houses in more than one city? Would you like to eventually retire from your full-time job? Anything is possible once you put your mind to it.

Determination is one of the keys to success. I did not stop after purchasing my first house in 1994. I set my personal goals to include these:

- I will be busy and not stagnant. I will stay active.

- I do not have a goal of owning a certain number of houses.

- One of my goals was to purchase a time-share. I did and I have a three-week timeshare at Marriott Vacation Club International.

- I would like to own an apartment in New York City. My husband once said in passing that he would like to have a place in New York. Of course I started looking right away! I am still looking for a good deal—they are quite costly.

Draft your plan on your computer, so it will be easy to add or revise your goals. If you do not have a computer, write it on your calendar and revise your plan every six months. You will then be able to indicate what you have accomplished in those six months, and what you will need to strive for in the six months ahead. You will be amazed at the results!

Maximize Your Rental

I have two, three, four, five, six and seven bedroom houses. I started buying houses with only a few bedrooms and quickly learned to only buy houses with five or more bedroom units to target the maximum earnings. I can rent one unit to three to five people. This gives me more leeway when renting. In other words, more rent can be charged because it is split evenly among more people. Renting houses in a summer resort town works to my advantage. Higher rents can be charged during the busy season, and when winter comes (slow season), I can take less, in terms of people and dollars. I make up for the slow season during the summer.

As I mentioned previously, it is very important to buy houses that have a minimum of two bathrooms. A one-bathroom house equals expense!

Make sure there is a driveway with enough parking for two vehicles or more. It is more convenient for the tenants, and more attractive when you are ready to sell the house.

Have a small backyard where people can sit outside and barbecue. Put in some flowering plants and shrubs. Perennials work the best, as you do not need to replant.

Location, Location, Location

By renting houses in the town of Newport, Rhode Island, I have accomplished the dream of many landlords. There are many reasons why people would want to rent a house in Newport. Aside from being a beautiful and friendly town, Newport is also a year-round community, and a summer vacation resort town located directly on the water.

Many of my tenants are summer visitors, and enjoy renting my homes because they are completely furnished and have added touches to make summer vacations more enjoyable. As I had briefly mentioned earlier in the book, I provide all the linens, towels, kitchenware, and other amenities that many summer rentals do not provide. Tenants that rent from me during the summer, return year and year. This makes my life, and my real estate agent's life, much much easier!

There are also two more bonuses, which the town of Newport offers to renters—Salve Regina University and a United States Naval Base are both located here. Since the college students basically rent from September through May, the houses are available for summer vacationers. Therefore, I am never "in-between" renters. As the summer season approaches, so do new renters!

My military tenants usually live in the house for approximately six months. If they are called away for military duty at another location, there is usually another tenant to take their place. The United States Navy men and women are my favorite tenants. They are always polite, pay on time, and keep the houses very tidy and clean.

When looking for a city or small town to buy houses to rent, keep in mind that the more opportunities the town has to offer, the more tenants will be looking for houses to rent!

Enjoy Yourself, Have a Sense of Humor, Keep Your Cool!

Having a positive attitude is the key to a stress-free job and working conditions. Six months after I became a landlord, many people approached me and said, "How is the landlord? Are you ready to give it up yet? You have so many problems. Do you want to sell your houses?" My answer from the start has been, "Problems are part of the business, solve them and do not brood over them." This holds true to this day.

When one of the maintenance personnel tells me about a problem I always say," Do not worry, everything will be fine. Let me take a look at it." I usually show them a solution. One said, "She is right!" When a problem arises, you have to train yourself to respond to the situation. You cannot wait for an hour, a few hours or the next day. You must find a solution immediately!

For example, I had tenants moving into one of the houses in a few days, and I had ordered some new kitchen cabinets to be delivered. The order was placed incorrectly, and the cabinets would not be at the house in time for the tenants' move-in date. I went to Home Depot and bought some kitchen cabinet doors to replace the rotten ones. It ended up costing us less money and they looked very nice. We then cancelled the original order.

"Keeping your cool" is another trait that a landlord needs to master. When I first started in 1994, I had some "bad apples" living in a few of the houses. I contacted the realtors to solve the problems. I went to court with these tenants many times. The second time I was in court, someone approached me with sound advice, which I followed. "Get yourself a lawyer." I still cannot remember this man's name and I would now like to publicly thank him with my whole heart.

At one of my houses, I felt that a few of the neighbors resented me because I am a woman and I am Oriental. One time there was a problem on one of the streets. One of the neighbors harassed me. He approached me, shouting at the top of his lungs, spewing out bad words. His face was three inches from mine, and his breath smelled like last week's garbage. I just stood there and let him expend his energy then I walked away from him. It is useless to argue. I just kept my cool.

Another incident happened on that same street. Another neighbor attacked me. This time I was in my car. He pounded and hit my car while screaming very loudly. I was thankful that my car was locked and I was safe inside. I called the police to report him. I just learned that he is a lieutenant in the fire department. He should be ashamed of himself the way he acted towards me.

A third incident happened when a woman neighbor came running out of her house screaming at me. She was yelling obscenities and saying that I rented the house to "other races." This particular house I had rented to construction workers who were building a hotel at the Naval Base. I don't know why she was so upset and throwing a fit!

Humor is something you cannot loose. You need humor to survive in this business. Remember to always have a smile on your face. I always greet my nice neighbors whenever I see them on the yard. I will sometimes knock on their door if I have not seen them for a while, just to say hello.

If your car breaks down, especially on the highway, you can loose your cool and humor. Since I started buying the houses, I have always driven a Subaru. This is my fourth one. Why Subaru? I want a car with four-wheel drive. I worry about the snow in my part of the country. I got the small Subaru, the Imprezza. If I buy a big car I will just have more junk in it. My car is my second office, and I tend to keep some paperwork, and supplies in it (among other things!)

According to my former roommate, Jean Li at Vassar College, I am reminded how a centrifuge works…If the content in the centrifuge is not balanced, it will shake. (This brings me back to my college days where I majored in chemistry.) Well, this is what was happening to my car. The car dealer did not listen to my description of the problem. They did not test-drive it, and when I picked it up from the dealership following service, it was still shaking. The tires were unbalanced. I decided to move to another Subaru dealer. This dealer test-drove my car when I had it serviced. I had told them that the car was shaking, they fixed the problem, and they now have my business.

If the properties are one to one and a half hours away from your residence do not be discouraged. After you have driven that far many times, it is just like going shopping.

I own several properties outside of Rhode Island. I have a wonderful travel agent to handle my plane reservations. She makes sure I always get the best deal. If she knows that a sale is near, she watches it and books it right away. She also handles the rental cars and hotels. I occasionally visit Hilton Head, South Carolina and Washington, DC. I visit my son in Washington to be sure he is cleaning his house!

Whatever the problem, I will always survive.

Keep Your Business Small

Even if you own ten houses, you do not have to hire managers and a complete line of maintenance personnel. You do not want to be doing payroll for a list of people. Have your accountant distribute a 1099 form at the end of the year, to those independent contractors to whom you have paid over $600.

As I mentioned earlier, I prefer to hire people to work for me part-time, who already have full-time jobs. It gives them extra money to earn, which helps out especially if they have a family. A person who already has a full-time job is usually more conscientious, hard working, and appreciates the fact that you have given him or her an opportunity to earn extra money.

Do Your Own Bookkeeping

Handling your own finances gives you more control and ability to better manage your money. Yes, you should hire an accountant to help you with your income taxes and to keep you updated on the latest rules and regulations in the tax world.

By paying your own bills, you can keep track and cross-reference every sales receipt and invoice that comes in. After all, you know better than anyone what purchases or repairs you have made, and can verify the costs and labor charges. If someone else is paying your bills, they will just pay everything that comes in. It is harder to dispute a claim or incorrect statement after the bill has already been paid. Again, it keeps you in control of the situation.

Do Not Be Afraid to Enter into Real Estate

Am I too old? Do I have enough money for a down payment? Will I be approved for a loan? What will happen if I do not find tenants? Am I getting in over my head?

I have but one statement to answer all of these questions. You will never know the answer unless you try. I did it. I started buying houses when I was forty-nine years old, I did not have a huge down payment, I was approved for a loan, and I found lots of tenants. Sometimes everything in life seems just too much. Just do it! You will not be sorry.

There is an old saying, "Do not put all of your eggs in one basket." Well I say, put one egg in real estate. You will be happy with the results. I once suggested to my son to invest some of his money in real estate as a down payment on another house. Everyone knows that sons never listen to their mothers. My son is no different. They all think that their mothers do not know anything, right Vince?

Give Good Service to Your Tenants

Your tenants are your number one priority. If my tenants are not happy, I am not happy and I do not get any sleep at night! Take care of all maintenance requests immediately, no matter how big or small.

Putting flowers in the yard, or on a deck or patio in the back of the house will make all the difference in the world to your tenants. Stop by to see them every now and then to see what they need. Do call first, to show the tenants that you are not "checking up on them."

Remember…service with a smile!

Appreciate Your Maintenance Crew and Real Estate Agents

You need to show your appreciation to your maintenance team and your realtors. These people are the core of your existence, without them you would have many many problems. (Without your realtor you would not even have any houses!!)

Take them out to lunch once in awhile, send them a note of thanks in appreciation. Give them a gift certificate or bonus at the end of the year. When someone goes the extra mile for you, you need to show your thanks.

Pay Your Bills

I would like to reinforce the importance of paying all of your bills on time. This includes paying your vendors, paying your credit cards, and paying your maintenance personnel in a timely manner. You cannot expect to get good service if you do not pay for it promptly.

You can make special arrangements with some vendors to invoice you monthly or every other month if that is easier on your bookkeeping. Once you establish a relationship with a vendor or maintenance personnel, they will go out of their way to help you if you are in a bind.

Examples of Real Estate Strategy

In 1980, I looked at a condominium near the mooring in Newport, Rhode Island. It had two bedrooms, two baths, two parking spaces, and the building had four floors with approximately sixty units. The price was $120,000 compared with my current condominium (which I ended up purchasing,), which cost $62,000. The price was almost double! I could have bought two units for the price. I shopped around, and found another house to buy!

In February of 2000, I looked at a house to buy. The description read something like, "Just off Bellevue Ave, walking distance to shopping, tennis matches, beach or harbor, excellent condition, well-maintained, large porch and off-street parking. The seller would entertain offers between $244,900 and $284,976. One of my realtors called to see if I wanted to view the house. As I entered the house, my brain immediately turned into a calculator.

I saw what was wrong, from the basement to the third floor, and estimated what the repairs would cost. The next day I made the offer of $240,000. I stuck to my price until the end of the negotiations. I think I may have insulted the owner, because they had an open house after I put in my bid. They had two offers. The other was $250,000, but the buyers did not have a mortgage approval yet. My realtor convinced them that her client was offering $10,000 less but that she was already approved for a mortgage. The negotiations went on for over three months.

These are the repairs I had to make before I could get a decent rental:

- Replace the boiler and the water heater with larger ones. (I do not like to get calls from tenants when there is not enough hot water.)
- Paint the inside of the house, and the trim on the outside.
- -Repair water stains on the ceiling.
- Repair the third floor ceiling, which was falling apart.
- -Sand all the floors.
- Caulk all the bathrooms.

The price of $284,876 was lowered to $275,000, when I saw the house at the end of February and decided to purchase it.

On the day of the closing, I had to inspect the house before I would sign the final papers. What do you know? The owners were still sleeping at 7:00 am. They should have already vacated and cleaned the house. There was so much rubbish that I told my lawyer to hold $500 at the closing, because I would have to hire someone to clean up the mess. I did not know that the owners were not coming to sign, and gave their realtor power of attorney to complete the transaction. Their realtor had no choice but to allow us to withhold the specified amount from his commission. I paid to have the house cleaned, and sent the remainder of the $500 back to the realtor in good faith.

Since all of my houses are fully furnished, I had furniture delivered the day after the closing. A young married neighbor harassed me on the street. She has since harassed me so many times that the other neighbors began to take notice. One of them said, "What a terrible, loud, unruly, hard disrespectful monster she is!" I just told this nice neighbor that my good qualities came out and that I was very calm and cool. The nasty woman neighbor said to me, "Why did you buy this house? You are making this neighborhood bad." I answered, "Why did you not buy this house yourself? They had a big For Sale sign in front for months!" I left her standing in the middle of the street.

Soon after I closed on my eighth house in 2001, my realtor asked me to look at a house on Broadway. It was huge. The house had the best flow design that I have seen so far. The floors are all hardwood. It has more repairs compared to the other five houses combined. The price was $269,000. The first floor was the only rentable unit. The rent was $600.00 per month. How in the world would I pay for the mortgage, unless I do some quick fixing? The house is a duplex, with five bedrooms in each unit. The following were the items that needed to be addressed:

- Replace three boilers and the water heater.
- Purchase kitchen cabinets, a sink and a range.
- Purchase all new appliances for both units.
- Repair the main sewer line.
- Sand the three floors.
- Paint the entire inside of the house.
- Install closets in four of the bedrooms.
- Purchase and install extras such as—blinds, valances, and pictures.

People who are just starting out would not be able to afford all of the repairs. Without the experience of working on the other houses, I would not have ventured into this project. I know that I have an excellent maintenance group, so I took the risk.

My maintenance personnel did a superb job with the painting. A local flooring company sanded the floors. They were preserved and in very good condition and they came out beautiful! I ordered new kitchen cabinets for the second floor, but the company never placed the order, so I went to Home Depot and ordered what we needed—lighting fixtures, bathroom fixtures, Formica, kitchen cabinets for both units, closets for the bedrooms. When we finished this project, I truly earned my degree from "Home Depot University!"

My maintenance personnel also found that we needed to change the third floor windows. I knew this would have to be done so I called my contact at the window shop I frequently use. Even without a deposit she ordered fifty-two windows for me. She had helped me with three of my other houses in the past.

I had one person doing the electrical wiring, two others did the plumbing and one of my maintenance personnel did the odds and ends like hanging the blinds, pictures and the curtain rods. Another installed the kitchen cabinets, closets and hung doors. My wonderful cleaning crew handled all of the cleaning. It took us six weeks to make this house livable!

I usually ask to paint prior to the closing, because the risk is little compared to fixing bathrooms or installing boilers, just in case the closing would not materialize.

There was a house in Newport that I considered buying. I took one of my maintenance personnel over to the house for an inspection prior to my closing the deal. He shook his head while we were in the basement, and he told me that the joists all had dry rot. He showed me what he meant by taking a screwdriver and punching several holes in the joists. The screwdriver went clear through the wood! It would cost a lot of to repair these supports to the house. We would have also had to install metal supports.

HILDA'S HINT

Working on a fixer-upper house is a good idea, especially if you have five to six rooms in each unit. The down side is that, it can drain your reserves fast, unless you refinance right away to replenish the reserves. You may need to call your mortgage coordinator or your bank frequently to complete the refinancing.

This man is one that I respect, admire and trust. His advice is always, "right on the mark!" I listen to it most of the time. I did not buy that house. I have no regrets, and feel good that I can count on such an experienced person whose advice and guidance can help me make the decision between buying and not buying a prospective rental property.

CHAPTER 9

Selling Property, Building a Primary Residence, Time Shares, Condominium

Selling Property

I purchased many properties over the years, made repairs when needed, and went through dozens of tenants, and yet have sold only one property, our primary residence. The driveway was very steep and the snowplow refused to plow it in the winter.

We stayed at this house for twenty years, and did our own shoveling in the winter, which was not easy. When it was plowed, the driver could not back up into the street safely.

When my son went off to college and we were getting a little older, I looked for a house with a flat driveway. We had purchased our original residence for $50,000 and we sold it for $157,000. The new owners did not care about the steep driveway, because they loved the house! We made a very good return on our initial investment and decided to build our own house, which you will read about later in this chapter.

I will touch briefly on the subject of selling a house, because I feel that this would not be a complete real estate guidebook without talking about selling a property. Personally, I do not buy houses, fix them up and then sell them to make a profit. If I did that, I would have nothing to do with my time. I enjoy the every-day details and the ups and downs of owning rental houses. There are times when I ask myself, why? But when the problem is resolved or I find new tenants or whatever the situation may be, I am still glad that I own rental houses.

Here are a few major points to remember when selling a house:

- Timing
- Appearance
- Price
- An Experienced Real Estate Agent

Timing

Timing is important, particularly if you live in an area that has a harsh winter season. Unless your job is transferred or you need to sell quickly for other reasons, it is best to wait until the spring season to put a house on the market. Buyers will not likely be looking for a house during a snowstorm or a thunderstorm, and your house will not be at its best during these periods anyway. Also, buyers will not want to move their children before the end of the school year.

HILDA'S HINT

Discuss with your real estate agent the best month to put your house on the market in the area where you are selling. Realtors are your best resource!

Appearance

The appearance of your house makes all the difference in the world to a prospective buyer. If there are two identical houses for sale in the same neighborhood, at nearly the same price, and one has nicer landscaping, which house has the advantage? The landscaped house of course. It appears to be well-kept, and prospective home owners, particularly first-time buyers, will be glad not to look forward to sinking money into landscaping costs. The more extras you can offer, such as landscaping,

HILDA'S HINT

Before putting a house up for sale, buy some fresh plants and flowers, paint the walls and remember to vacuum the rugs!

a deck or patio, nice appliances and fresh paint, the more likely a buyer will choose your house.

HILDA'S HINT

Even in a recession or if the housing market is not doing well in your area, there are still many reasons to sell and for people to buy houses. Remember people will always need a nice place to live. It may as well be the house you are selling!

Pricing

Many factors are involved in pricing a house to sell. Your realtor can tell you the selling prices of other houses in the area; the house appraisal, and what you owe on the loan are also involved in determining the price. Remember that the nicer your house appears, the more upgrades and extras you have added, and how the house is decorated, are all important in the pricing decision.

You want to make a profit. Therefore, the more you put into a house, the higher the profit! It is a simple equation…you need to spend money to make money!

Real Estate Agent

We have discussed earlier in the book the importance of an experienced and competent real estate agent. Agents stand to make a good deal of money in commissions on house sales, therefore, they will try everything humanly possible to sell your house. Well, most of them will. You must trust your agent because he or she could be the difference between a sale and no sale.

The Tax Deferred Exchange

If a property is sold within one year, the house can qualify for a tax-deferred exchange.

Once a property is sold, the seller has forty-five days to purchase a property anywhere in the U.S. The seller must close on the property within one hundred and eighty days in order to qualify for the tax-deferred exchange.

I usually buy houses to keep them long-term. Due to some avoidable circumstances, one house that I recently bought needed to be sold immediately. The location was not ideal for a rental property, although it was perfect for residential, and it was a fixer-upper.

The exterior of the house was power-washed, allowing the beauty of the red cedar shingles to show. Our maintenance man painted the outside trim and the interior of the house. The floors were sanded, and a plumber repaired the faucets in the bathroom and kitchen, and replaced the sump pump. New gutters were installed, and our carpenter repaired missing red cedar shingles and soffits, and fixed the small roof over the basement. He called to inform me that the wood panel to the entrance of the basement was rotten and the previous estimate he had given me for the repairs would not cover this problem. He said, "I know the house is being sold. What would you like me to do?" I replied, "If it is still in my domain…it must be fixed! I believe in the saying, "What goes around, comes around". Doing these repairs will bring me good luck and will enable a quick sale.

HILDA'S HINT

If the house is a fixer-upper, you will need money for repairs. Make the necessary repairs and then sell the house to qualify for a tax-deferred exchange, which will save capital gains taxes on the transaction. (Please see Appendix for more information on tax-deferred exchanges.)

Buying a Residential Lot and Building a Home

Two years before my son left for college, I started looking for a house to buy. Most of the houses that I saw either had steep driveways or the interiors needed remodeling. I was not interested in shoveling snow again, or taking the time to remodel a house to make it livable. I then looked at lots for building a house. I saw one lot with an asking price of $65,000, but he wanted to put only $40,000 in the paper. I did not like it and felt it would be a losing proposition. My accountant, Richard Hoopis told me to keep looking until I found something that I liked.

For the three years previous, I went to home shows and I saw a company called Deck House. I liked their style of contemporary houses and they offered all the qualifications that I needed along with the peace of mind of the builder that Deck House would choose. Before I bought the lot, I asked Dave Vaniccola from Deck House to look at some other lots with me, and to give me a rating on which ones he thought would be the best one for my home. He chose the same lot that my accountant had suggested. However, it had a steep driveway. I told Dave that I would let him build me a Deck House provided that it had a flat driveway. He said that he could do it. I was impressed.

My husband and I considered the different house plan options, decided which ones we liked, and signed the contract. I told my husband that he could not change his mind because it would cost us money and a delay on the project. I obtained a construction loan through GMAC, which saved me many sleepless nights. The builder was then paid by the bank, only on what was "nailed to the house."

When we contracted Deck House to build our house, they offered us a package, including appliances from Miele Appliances, and cabinets for the bathrooms and kitchen from Imperia Cabinet Corporation. Because Deck House orders in large volume from these companies, the savings are passed on to their clients. The only outside contractor we needed to hire was a local landscaper. They installed plenty of loam— you should see how the shrubs and trees have flourished!

During construction I noticed that the garage was in the skeleton stage and I asked the builder about it? He said, "It is not included in the estimate." I called Deck House and they informed me that it was not included in the original building estimate. Can you imagine that this woman getting to be like a shark! I asked, "How much to finish the garage?" They told me it would cost $2,000 for completion, which I agreed to.

I had air conditioning installed with some other extras including a dehumidifier and filters. If I installed it later, it would cost more. I also had all of the bathrooms and the hardwood floors installed and completely finished. I was thinking of the eventual resale value, and included many additional extras in the house. I had a Jacuzzi installed, which we have never even used! Again, this was another added extra that will attract buyers someday.

Another problem arose regarding the bank's estimate of the amount that was to be paid to the builder for one month of services. The bank had refused to pay him for the wood flooring that was delivered because it was not "nailed to the house." The builder insisted that he had to pay $385.00 in interest. The estimator said, "Well, you can ask Mrs. Erfe to pay it." The builder charged me $385.00, which I paid just to end the argument.

Thereafter, I watched costs, and the builder, like a hawk! I later considered this builder for a project in Newport. His estimates were outrageous, and that was the end of our working relationship!

Upon completion of the house, Deck House gave me a ten-year warranty, which I used when there was a water leak drip onto the floor. I called customer service, and they sent a roofer to assess the problem. Apparently, the original roofer had missed some flashing that was causing the leak. The roofer fixed the leak and the problem was immediately solved.

Overall, I am satisfied with Deck House, and we receive many compliments on our home.

What I learned from working with Deck House made my job easier when I worked on rental houses in Newport.

I called them recently to ask if they could help me with the paint on the house. The people that originally painted the house did not leave a sample of the can or the name of the paint. I just wanted to put it on file. I received a disconcerting answer from them. I never experienced this attitude before from Deck House. I am currently negotiating on buying a lot in Newport and I intend to ask Deck House to build the house. Has their attitude changed? I guess I will soon find out!

Hilton Head Condominium

For our retirement during the winter months, we purchased an ocean view condominium in South Carolina at the Hilton Head Island Beach and Tennis Resort. The owners operate the resort themselves under the management of CVC Corporation Board of Directors. Because of the disastrous occurrences of September 11, 2001 and other factors creating uncertainty, the management company now covers itself with long-term agreements.

I always try to make sure that our condominium is in superior condition to generate higher rent, and the management company's rental division keeps us updated on the condition of our unit. The resort has vacationers from the Northeast, who escape the winter cold, and they usually stay on Hilton Head from November to April, so we rent to them on a monthly basis, although tenants also rent for a few days or weeks at a time.

I am so saddened that Lillian Seigler lost her job at the complex. She served the complex and the owners with her full support. It is a big loss to the resort!

We have owned the unit since 1980 and have spent only five vacations there. The woman in charge of the rental operations department is very efficient, informative and resourceful. I have developed a good relationship with her and the rest of the rental department, and I am confident that when I cannot get to

Hilton Head, they will take care of the unit for me. They inform me on what is needed to upgrade the unit, like needing new furniture, painting, or changing the wallpaper, and necessary repairs.

Two years ago I went to visit the condominium because the rental operations agent told me it needed refurbishing. I arrived around midnight and when I entered the unit I immediately knew what she meant. The next day I talked to the people that she had contacted to do the job, and I signed the contract for the painters, and I bought some new furniture. I went to Wal-Mart to buy kitchenwares, a set of pots and pans, a few small appliances, a microwave, a coffee maker, and a can opener. It was very easy to shop because I have been doing it for the houses in Newport. I did not even need to make a list, I knew it by heart. I went to the factory outlets to buy linens, a new comforter and other items we needed for the bedrooms. I also picked up some wall decorations to complete the job.

A friend of mine came with me. She loved Hilton Head because the shrimp season just started. We cooked various Philippine shrimp dishes for dinner and had a wonderful time!

The condominium in Hilton Head Island is well worth our original investment. You cannot buy this unit now for the original price, particularly with an ocean view. We originally purchased the unit for $89,000, furnished. It is now worth an amazing $250,000!

Hilton Head is a family friendly resort. It is a nice feeling to see families vacationing here at our condominium even if it is only for one or two weeks. It is economical for a family to vacation on Hilton Head. If they stay for one week, they have seven days to spend money on hotels, condos or houses, restaurants, and shopping. If they rent for one month and only come on the weekends, they will only spend money for about three days a week.

The town of Newport, on the other hand, does not like houses to be rented by the week. They prefer monthly rentals and rentals for the entire summer season, as well as year-round rentals. If the monthly renters come three days a week or only on weekends, then Newport is losing four days of business from them. I can understand the Realtors Association's view on this matter. If the town would allow weekly rentals for families, they will encourage more families to come and not lose the other 4 days of income for the town's businesses. It is difficult for mothers and fathers who have to work to support their families to be away from work for a month at a time.

Timeshare at Grand Ocean Resort

I have a two-week per year timeshare platinum at the Marriott's Grand Ocean Resort in Hilton Head Island, South Carolina. Platinum refers to the time of year that we have our weeks, which in our case is June through August. In early 1990's, I went to Hilton Head to inspect our condominium and meet the maintenance personnel handling the remodeling of the unit. I brought a friend with me, and while wandering around the island we stopped for lunch at the Marriott Hotel, where we saw an advertisement about a timeshare resort. I spoke to the gentleman in the office who refused to give me a presentation because my husband was not with me. We argued about their policy and my friend and I said they were discriminatory against women. I think he suspected that I wanted the free dinner that you got after listening to the presentation. I told him that I would look into the government policy on this matter. The gentleman must have been taken aback because he gave us the presentation and showed us the main site.

Let me briefly explain a timeshare. Timeshare means that you own a week of use of a condominium or townhouse, usually at a resort destination, each year. With Marriott, if you are in the Platinum Club, you can choose your week during a specific period of time. You can use your week as vacation time for yourself, or rent it to someone else

I called my husband and told him about the timeshare. Of course, he said, "No!" I am so accustomed to his answers, and I eventually bought the two-week timeshare. I always rely on my own good judgment. Certainly it made that gentleman's day worth the effort of giving us the presentation.

Marriott Corporation required a 20% down payment and would give financing for the remaining 80% for ten years. I put the 20% down and did get the financing from them for ten years. It is just like paying installments when purchasing a car. I rent the weeks during summer season, I list it for rent twelve or thirteen months ahead to get a popular week, and the excellent customer service department accommodates any questions.

Susan Deschene of the Marriott Vacation International has been my contact all these years. She helps me to tackle any problem, large or small and gives me a solution every time! The value of the condo has gone up since I bought the weeks. I also get good rent when we cannot vacation there.

Susan has provided me with some basic information on a timeshare.

"A timeshare is a deeded or Right-to-Use ownership of real estate for a specified duration of time. Through this ownership, it provides club exchange opportunities for vacation usage at other club resorts, or, through Interval International, exchange options, usage at a number of other affiliated resorts throughout the world; thus providing flexibility and a variety of vacation experiences.

Points are accumulated through promotions, special offers, incentives, sweepstakes, and Marriott credit card usage.

There are four "seasons" offered. Gold and Platinum are the most desirable seasons based on activities offered, such as skiing in Aspen, and the beaches at Grande Ocean

"Silver" is the next most desirable season, followed by "Bronze" the least desirable, off- season.

Timeshare at Custom House

Marriott sends letters to prospective buyers about seminars they are holding. The letter indicates how you can use the points you have accumulated. If you are a good client of Marriott Hotels or you are in the Marriott Vacation Club, you receive points for every dollar that you spend in the Marriott Company. This includes hotels, restaurants, conventions, buying timeshares, and more. If I buy a one-week timeshare, I get 120,000 points. I can redeem these points for an airline ticket, hotel nights or whatever the package may offer. One letter I received from Marriott mentioned a presentation on their new urban development project called The Custom House, in Boston, Massachussetts. My husband suggested we take a closer look at this timeshare. Of course, I bought a week, and I rent it out too. The value of the unit has gone up and it is a very profitable rental property.

Marriott contacted me several times to talk to other perspective buyers for The Custom House. I am very good at showing them the advantages of owning one of these units. I have also profited from and obtained airline tickets, Marriott hotel stays, rental cars, and cruises from earning points. Belonging to this time share has been very beneficial in these other ways in addition to collecting rent.

We have owned the time share for ten years and we have used the Grande Ocean only once. It is on the waterfront, beautiful and has wonderful warm ocean water. My son had used Custom House several times. In the near future, I will probably not buy another timeshare until my husband says he is ready to go on vacation again. He has been mostly using his vacation time visiting his folks in the Philippines.

Condominium in Arlington

After my son's graduation from college, he got a job in the Washington DC area. He intended to share an apartment or house with two of his friends. The two roommates backed out of the plans, and my son was on his own.

I contacted a realtor in Newport to help me locate a realtor in the D.C. and Virginia area who would show us reasonably priced apartments. I limited the apartment hunting to three days, between 8:00 a.m. and 5:00 p.m., as we were limited on time and funds, and needed to find something as soon as possible. When we arrived in Arlington, the agent was ready for us and promptly showed me her list of apartments.

During the first three hours of searching, we were discouraged, as the rents were outrageous. My son really needed to have one or two roommates to afford these prices. I told the realtor that we should probably start looking for something to buy, and we went back to her office. I called my mortgage coordinator, in Rhode Island and I asked her to see how much my son could be approved for in terms of a mortgage. I gave her his salary information and she went right to work for us. My son was going to carry his own mortgage and be responsible for it—his first lesson in the real world. We found a condominium with a reasonable asking price, located in a convenient area. The realtor thought that I would make a low offer, although I only offered $4,000 less than the asking price. She was very surprised. I saw that there was nothing that needed to be repaired in the unit, however, I did notice a dirty rug that needed shampooing!

My son's condominium complex is seven stories tall, with underground parking and a swimming pool. It is very quiet, and within walking distance to the Hilton Hotel and the subway, making it easy for him to get to work. The building is surrounded by townhouses in the upper $500,000 range.

As soon as we closed the deal for my son, my mortgage coordinator contacted GMAC in the Virginia area to start the paperwork. This was yet another surprise to the realtor, because she had told us to go to the bank to get a mortgage. I informed her that we were all set and my son was approved.

Without the previous experience I had with the real estate market, he would have probably ended up with a different deal and we would have wasted a lot of time looking at more places.

Next Stop, the Big Apple!

When in New York City recently, I read in the real estate section of *The New York Times* magazine about homes in the city. My husband and my brother left me alone to look at some possibilities.

On Monday morning, August 20, 2001 at 9:00 am, I started calling the ads that I was interested in from the magazine. Some of the realtors were not in or they were still on vacation, therefore I left messages. I got an answer from one company and we made an appointment to meet at 11:45 a.m. I walked to First Avenue and I saw the United Nations building. As I was a bit early, I walked around for a while. I saw another billboard with an ad for another building. I went into the office and asked for some information, and was asked to fill in a form with my personal information. I gave them my last business card, which had some writing on it and requested the receptionist to copy it, as it was my last card. She was very nice, copied it and put it with my application. I made an appointment to meet with an agent at 1:00 p.m. I then left to go to the 11:45 a.m. appointment.

When I arrived at the office, I gave my card to the agent and requested to have it copied. She gave me a tour of the office and then showed me how the building would look, and the design of the different units and the prices. The women were very nice and explained the project explicitly.

I was still early for the 1:00 p.m. appointment, so I walked around towards the United Nations Building. I came upon another building that was under construction and they also had a big sign showing where you could inquire about the units. I headed toward Second Avenue and Forty-Eighth Street. I went into the office and told the receptionist that I saw the sign on First Avenue and I wanted to inquire about the building. I proceeded to tell her that I was interested in buying a place in New York City. She said, " I am very busy."

I looked around and there was nobody around except the security guard. I continued to tell her that I had only one business card and asked her to copy it. She again said, "I am very busy and I have a lot of things to do." I did not budge from that spot until she copied it. I suggested that she should also copy the back of the card to show that I am a serious buyer. She told me that it was not necessary. I then asked her if I needed to complete any application or form about myself as was customary. The receptionist said with disdain, " We do not have anything like that here." I asked her for her name. She hesitated for a long time and did not answer me. I told her that I would not leave the office until I got her name. She finally told me her name and I wrote it down.

There was a big sign on her reception desk that stated, "We do not discriminate against any race, color, or ethnicity."

I felt that she discriminated against me because I am Oriental. She probably thinks that I have a lot of guts to come in here, especially since it is Donald Trump's building. I left, and returned after a few minutes. When I came back, the guard said, " Somebody is giving the receptionist trouble." He was talking about me and was about ready to throw me out. I told the receptionist, "I am giving you my cellular number, just in case somebody has time to give me information about the building. I do not leave for Rhode Island until 5:00 p.m. and I have time."

Up to this date, she never called me back nor did anyone else in that organization. Who do you think is the loser in this case? The receptionist and the guard are on salary, so they do not lose anything. *It is Mr. Trump who lost my business!* What if ten Orientals came in and they all got the receptionist's discriminatory attitude. A sale is a sale. It is good to have contact information for the people coming into the office for future reference. They might buy another property from another project of Mr. Trump's. No matter how big your organization, employing a person with this woman's attitude can topple any project.

I continued walking around before my next appointment, and I saw William B. May Real Estate Company. I went in and inquired. They were very nice and I was assigned a realtor. I gave them the same deal that I had given the receptionist about the business card, and the realtor handled everything. Within five minutes, he showed me two apartments at 100 United Nations Plaza. I told him that I had an appointment at 1:00 p.m. and told him which building. He knew the building, which was called Beekman Regent. He telephoned them and he came with me to look at the unit. I loved it! It was very New York. The sales manager who helped us that day was very nice and accommodating.

After a month, the realtor had made several other appointments for me to see a few more units. The last place was another Trump project, 220 Riverside Boulevard, near the Hudson river. As soon as I entered the office, the receptionist gave me two information sheets to complete. When I was finished I told her, "This is very unusual. You are having me fill out these forms and when I went to the other Trump office, the woman did not have me fill out any forms. This receptionist was very cordial and responded, "You need to complete the forms so we will be able to keep records of who came into the office." I also loved this place.

My first appointment was at Grand Beekman on First Avenue, which was under construction. A sales representative showed me the sample of how the unit would look.

Another realtor faxed me information on several units. A third realtor also sent me several choices. I have spoken to them only on the phone, because I cannot get back to New York for now. I have been "thrown a curve" in my usual routine. My husband recently lost his secretary, and who fills her shoes, me! I will return to New York in the spring to continue my search, when his new secretary can handle the work.

CHAPTER 10 Hilda's Way to Investment Success

The Little Things that Mean a Lot to Tenants

When I had only ten to fifteen Navy officers as tenants, I usually invited them to a Chinese-Philippine dinner at my home. They all drove to my house even though it was about an hour away in Lincoln, Rhode Island. However, now that I have twenty-five to forty tenants, I bring them all to a Chinese restaurant in Newport for a fabulous buffet. The Chinese buffet opened about three years ago, and we have been going there ever since. Because the navy officers are in Newport for only six months, I usually have two groups of them per year, therefore we visit the Chinese buffet twice each year.

I take my tenants out to dinner to say, "thank-you" for being my tenants and for taking good care of my houses. You cannot believe the appreciation and kind words that I receive from them. They have told me that no other landlord has ever treated them this way. It gives me extreme satisfaction to hear these words, and I, in turn, tell them how grateful that I am to have them living in my houses.

If I am in the Newport area around lunchtime, I will sometimes bring my tenants pizza and pizza nuggets from a local pizzeria in Providence. Pizza is always a big hit! The local pizzeria takes special care with my orders. I also do this during the summer months so I can get to know my summer tenants a little better. When I have summer tenants, they are always happy and appreciative of my thoughtfulness. I also like to treat my realtors to a pizza party every now and then, especially if I learn that it is one of their birthdays!

One year, one of the navy officer tenants told me that his birthday was the following week. I brought him a chocolate cake with candles. He loved it! I had made the right choice, and had also made a friend for life! Once when I was in the Philippines, my realtor called me long distance to inform me that she rented one house to five Navy officers and gave me the details of the lease. Before hanging up the phone, she told me she was celebrating her fortieth birthday. I congratulated her and said I would bring her something special from the Philippines.

HILDA'S HINT

Treat your tenants to dinner or lunch throughout the year as a 'thank-you'. It is genuinely appreciated, and it gives you a chance to get to know your tenants and their families.

I also give a little something to each person on my maintenance team—I do not like to just give them a Christmas card, so I thought of giving them a gift certificate to the Chinese buffet restaurant. Most of them called me with their great appreciation. This was a gift they could share with their family.

Getting Involved in the Community

Someone recruited me for the Council for International Visitors. This organization sponsors international students who are attending the Peace Keeping class at the Navy Justice School in Newport. The course is designed to bring international participants in contact with the American values of generosity, justice, fairness and equality. A US sponsor acts as a citizen diplomat and has a very important role. I have had many Naval Officer tenants over the years. I feel that this is one way to give them something in return.

When I joined, I was assigned to Lt. Colonel Zulkipli Sanni, a commanding officer from Sarawak, Malaysia; and LTC Ramie Adel-Fattah Halawa, from Egypt. When I attended the welcome reception, I also met a student from the Philippines, Deputy Commander Ernesto Baylon of the Armed Forces of the Philippines. I also had the privilege to meet his wife, Dr. Norma Baylon. I brought them to the factory outlets and helped them buy things to take home. I took them to some historical places and around the town of Newport to see some of the sights. I introduced the Chinese buffet idea to one of the other sponsors, and we all went to dinner there together, which was very pleasant.

I met Colonel Baylon in the Philippines when I went home for a visit, and I invited him to our town fiesta. This was a wonderful way to build our friendship. The Babylons sent us a beautiful Christmas lantern, which will be on display this coming holiday season in the front of our house.

The following year, another class came in and the organization asked me again to host another student. Of course, I said yes. There were no Malaysian students, so I was given two Egyptian students to sponsor. I took them on a shopping expedition along with a fourth student and his sponsor.

I brought them to the Vanity Fair Factory Outlets in North Darmouth, Massachusetts. I helped each one of them buy items until all of the shopping carts were full. They even had a specific price range they wanted to adhere to, no more than $15.00 an item. We truly got some bargains that day! Included in this group were: Brigadier General Shaker Ismail Mash Salaam; LTC Tamer Ahmed Maher, LTC Mohamed Abdel Fattah and LTC Mahmoud El Shafie. The last group I sponsored had a Filipino captain Eufrocio Regodon, and a Malaysian major, Razif Ramli.

HILDA'S HINT

There are many things that you can do to get involved in your town. Ask a City Hall representative or your local realtor for information about volunteering for a community project or hosting a foreign visitor. And remember that the more you give, the more you will receive.

The other Egyptian sponsors invited my husband and I together with the four Egyptian officers for dinner at their lovely home. This was a wonderful experience to learn about another country, and to teach these men about our wonderful country.

I have learned how to deal with many different types of people while being a landlord. This certainly gave me a lot of experience when hosting the foreign visitors. It is good to be involved with the community where your rental houses are located.

Love Thy Neighbors

Neighbors are an integral part of owning real estate. When I am looking for a house to buy I first think, would I like to retire in this house? With this thought, I always check to be sure that I buy a house in a nice neighborhood.

Some of the neighbors like me, and some do not. The neighbors that like me show appreciation and compliment me on how I have made improvements to the house. I usually give them a tour of the inside of the house and show them the landscaping around the house, to show how much work we have done. They are pleased because the nicer my house looks, the nicer the neighborhood looks. It is a give-and-take situation.

There are other neighbors who just do not like me—why I do not know. When I purchased my third house, one of my maintenance personnel was inspecting the house and a neighbor approached him and said, "Well that Jap is buying everything!" My maintenance person was quick to realize that this neighbor was talking about me! He replied, "She is not a "Jap," she is from the Philippines. So what if she likes to buy houses. Mind your own business. Why don't you buy one yourself if you are so concerned?" He is always alert and protects his work and those who work with him. I work very hard and the freedom to do good work is very uplifting to me. If these people only realized that I know how to help them build their own wealth.

When he told me about what the neighbor had said, I took it as a compliment. Whenever I vacation with my mother and my sisters, I see loads of Japanese tour buses every place that we go. Some people have the money to do this. That neighbor forgot that other people also exist in America. Even when you buy a house, you still have to pay the mortgage.

As I mentioned in an earlier chapter, Newport has strict ordinances concerning noise pollution. I take every possible step to solve the noise problems in my houses. Over the years I have learned to give the realtors the task of interviewing all prospective tenants, and alerting them of the ordinances in Newport. The only tenants I personally interview are the students.

One year I met our tenants for the summer condominium rental. I went to our condominium and introduced myself to the tenants, and noticed they had brought all new furniture with them, some still in the original boxes from the store. I asked them why they brought furniture, because I was having new furniture delivered the following week. I had ordered four twin beds, a living room set, and six new chairs for the dining room table. I normally change the condominium's furniture every three to four years to spruce things up a bit. The tenants told me that one of the neighbors told them that I furnished all of my houses with furniture I took out of the garbage! Well, I thought to myself, who throws out furniture in the garbage and where would I even get it? The tenants proceeded to tell me that this neighbor said another landlord had put a couch on the curb to be thrown out and that they saw one of my maintenance men take the couch to our condominium.

After researching this story, I discovered that some of the previous student tenants took the couch to the condo for their own use. It was then discarded prior to when they moved out. I felt that this neighbor was very unjust in spreading rumors because they did not even know the correct facts of the story.

I require all my tenants to meet their neighbors. This is for common courtesy purposes, and for emergencies. Also, since all of the neighbors have my contact information, they can inform me when there are any valid problems.

City Hall

A landlord has many dealings with the town hall or city hall as part of the job. I am lucky that the City Hall in Newport has many wonderful employees who take pride in their jobs and are always willing to lend a helping hand. The business manager and the solicitor were very helpful to me during a time when I was having problems with tenants' violations, giving me pointers on how to deal with them. They told me to build a good relationship with the local realtors, which I had already started to do. I think they helped me because I am a taxpayer and it is part of their job. If I am successful in my business ventures in Newport, then I can bring good things into the town.

I also love the Newport Water Department meter supervisors. They are always there when I need them, especially in an emergency. One winter, a neighbor of one of my tenants, saw water gushing from the house. She immediately called the Water department and they came right away and closed off the main line until my maintenance personnel could come to fix the problem. The pipe had frozen and eventually burst. In one of my other houses, the tenants saw water in the basement and called the maintenance personnel. The main water line from the street needed to be changed, and the Newport Water Department immediately came and shut off the main line. They also returned to open the main line once our plumber had repaired the problem.

The Municipal Court clerk is another employee who has been extremely helpful when I went to City Hall to get some parking stickers and guest passes for my tenants and I presented my driver's license as proof of residence. Since I do not live in Newport, I was given "the third degree" of why I needed the stickers and passes. Most of these employees did not know me, as I usually deal with the same person. The clerk immediately told these employees, "She has many properties in Newport." She and I had gotten to know each other after I had made many trips to City Hall during the time of my problems with the tenants' violations. She told me that City Hall should provide me with an office in their building!

The other county clerks have always helped me with the yearly registration of the houses. At least two of them help each other to complete the paperwork for the registration, so I do not have to wait for a long time.

The tax collector is also a good person to befriend! When I purchased eight recycling bins, he was very nice and helped me bring them to my car. The employees in the tax collection office always give me a big smile whenever I see them.

Dress for Success

When I go into Newport I usually dress very casually. I prefer to wear pants because I am constantly going up and down stairs and into the basement and up to the third floor. I will do this many times a day, especially if I am inspecting one of the houses. A skirt would be fine to wear, but I am afraid that I would trip over it! I never wear work boots, but will wear my trusty snow boots during bad winter weather. I feel that the boots are cumbersome and prefer wearing the rubber-soled shoes. I feel much safer. I prefer Nike sneakers and Bass shoes. They especially keep me dry while I am working in the basement!

I always check the basement to see if there are any water leaks coming from the boiler. I will also check to be sure that everything is clean and there is no extra debris lying around. If a house contains any asbestos in the insulation, I have a licensed technician remove it, after purchasing the house.

When meeting prospective tenants or showing someone one of my properties, I dress smart but still casual. If a realtor were showing one of the houses, I would also expect him or her to dress neatly as well. After all, they represent me.

CHAPTER 11 My Newport, Rhode Island, Experience

I felt that this book would not be complete if I did not include the comments of some of my business associates and tenants. I wrote each of them a short letter about my new project, of writing a book on buying and renting houses. Asking each to write an essay on our business dealings and how we work together. I asked the tenants to write about their experiences living in my houses, or whatever else they wanted to write. I am indebted to friends, business associates and tenants who responded. Everyone had a different version of their experience living in one of my houses or working with me. I could not have asked for more!!! They are all great and I thank each one of them from the bottom of my heart.

High-Fives from Business Associates and Tenants

Dear Friends:

I first began working with the Erfes in 1995. After doing their personal construction loan on their personal residence, I took a look at their entire real estate portfolio. Hilda's goal was to build a portfolio of real estate that would yield sufficient income and asset growth, to eventually become a significant contributor to their retirement income. We quickly got to work to help them attain that goal. Real estate investing is a long-term commitment having to deal with mortgages, tenants, and the art of managing and assessing cash flow.

The Erfes had a small portfolio of real estate when I first met them. The properties were all in excellent rental areas such as Newport, Rhode Island, which attracted the Navy, monthly vacationers and college students. The Erfes decided what type of tenants they wanted to house, and bought properties that would yield the highest and most consistent rental income coupled with the properties attractive toward appreciation. On average, the Erfes purchased one to two houses per year to continue adding to their portfolio. Because the property selections were limited to single family, condominiums and two-family properties, the mortgage rates and terms have always been the most favorable. Upon doing a complete analysis of their property, we quickly went to work to refinance the portfolio.

The plan for their retirement quickly went into play, at a time that the rates were favorable. The goal was to bring all the existing mortgages from their existing thirty-year term down to a fifteen-year term, as well as reducing the existing interest rates on all of the properties. By bringing all the existing properties to fifteen to twenty-year terms, they will accrue principal (equity) quicker and will be close to being paid off at the time of retirement. All closing costs were included in the new principal balances of the loans so additional funds were not needed to refinance the properties. We were able to take advantage of the existing equities in the properties. When developing a long-term real estate investing plan, it is very important to make sure that you have a personal mortgage banker that is informed of the plan, so that the sections of products, rates and terms will coincide with the goals of the investing plan.

It was during this time that Hilda continued to add to their portfolio. Hilda was informed of down payment requirements needed to get the best rate and term for the specific property being purchased. The down payment is based on property's purchase price, or the appraised value, whichever is less.

A minimum of 20% down payment is needed to avoid Private Mortgage Insurance. Private Mortgage Insurance, known also as PMI, is required when a borrower puts less than 20% or 30% on the purchase price, depending on the number of units or exact guidelines from the lender or investor. Multiple guidelines are used to arrive at the program specific guidelines for each and every purchase.

You should never let interest rates prevent you from buying a great long-term investment. As real estate values continue to appreciate (in most cases), the rates are very cyclical and always moving. If interest rates are out of favor, it is wise to go with the lowest closing cost and higher term, and plan to refinance the property to a lower rate and shorter term when the rates are more favorable. At all times it is important to maintain current values and interest rates and run numbers when the rates take a dip. By having a team of attorneys, appraisers and mortgage bankers that know your plan, you will be able to bring together professionals familiar with their line of business who can direct the investor as to the best course of action.

There are many different ways to purchase investment properties these days. The location and the number of units on the property will determine the final loan to value. It is important to remember that the higher the loan to value, the higher the risk, which usually is followed by higher interest rates, points or higher mortgage insurance rates. Any residential properties that have five or more residential units, or have mixed use or commercial attached to them, are considered commercial properties.

Looking at varieties of individual products can send your mind into a tailspin. It is best to give all the details to your mortgage professional, and allow them to search and choose the best mortgage program for your given situation. Products vary from 100% financing, which will often come as a 75% first and a 25% second, or an 80% first and a 20% second mortgage. Investor Rehab loans have also become more popular over the past few years. It is always a good investment, if the numbers work well with a minimum investment on the borrowers part. There is also 90% loan to value product available as a single mortgage, with very competitive rates.

When searching for the best product for yourself it is important to ask yourself a few questions. First question would be, "how long do you want to keep the house?" If your answer is long term, then higher down payment and shorter terms will yield more favorable rates, and in the long run you will gain a higher return on your initial investment. If your answer is short term, then the less cash investment the better, and the higher rate is less relevant, because the expected term will be short. The next question should be, "how much of my personal funds can I tie up in an investment property?" If you are planning on purchasing multiple properties, then it is always best to keep the cash on reserve, and go with a higher loan to value product. Maybe a seller would consider holding financing at a favorable interest rate for a certain rate and term.

It is important to have a plan of actions prior to any investing. Select locations that would not be difficult to sell, if you need to turn your assets into cash. Have a long term and a short-term financial plan in the works, so you have a road map to measure your success. And most of all treat it like a business and you'll be guaranteed to make money.

Lynn M. LaFontaine
Vice President
Trident Mortgage Corporation
11373 Wampanoag Trail
East Providence, Rhode Island 02915

(Marguerite thought it would be informative if she explained the various loans offered by Credit Unions.)

Credit Union Central Falls offers several different types of mortgages. They offer Residential, Commercial, Equity Loan, HELOC, and from single family all the way up to four-family homes, condominiums, with owner-occupied to non-owner occupied.

The credit union offers fixed rate mortgages; - 10, 15, 20, and 30 years with no points, 1 point and two points. Plus, they offer a wide array of variable rate mortgages with different terms.

The application fees are as follows:

— Single Family: $350.00
— 2-4 Family: $400.00
— Construction: $500.00

*Save $100.00 by putting our sign on land/property for financed by CUCF

The types of mortgages we have are as follows:

— Single Family Homes
— 1-2-3-4 Family Owner Occupied
— 1-2-3-4 Family Non Owner Occupied
— Construction Mortgages
— Land Mortgages with 30% down required
— TurnKey Mortgages
— Commercial Mortgages

The amount down is as follows:

— 10% down 90% financing
— 20% down 80% financing

On 20% down, the member can either pay the taxes or have CUCF pay them. With 10% down CUCF, will pay the taxes.

Time Frames: — Purchases usually 4-6 weeks or later depending on the P & S
— Refinances 6-8 weeks
— Equity Mortgages and HELOC 4-6 weeks

Items you need to bring in most cases:

— Refinances and purchases
— Two years previous tax returns with W-2's attached
— 4 most recent pay stubs showing year to date figures
— Homeowner's policy and tax bill
— Most recent mortgage statements (ref)
— Three months complete bank statements
— Purchases: P & S agreement signed by both parties
— Copy of the down payment sheet on current house, showing taxes and other pertinent information.
— Any assets: 401(k), IRA's, mutual funds etc.
— Any outstanding bills
— Any other items on request

Also on HELOC the rate is based on the Prime Rate and is a variable rate mortgage. Minimum payment is either $200.00 or 1.50% of the unpaid balance. Check writing ability for major purchases and available on owner-occupied one to four family dwellings.

The only other fees to members on refinances and purchases are the attorney's fees.

Marguerite Vadnais
Credit Union Central Falls
Cumberland, Rhode Island 02864

We have been working with Hilda for several years. When Hilda is driving around the state, usually Newport, Rhode Island, I receive a telephone call from her indicating that she is considering purchasing a piece of property. She then gives me some information, just to start things moving. Once she definitely decides she will purchase the property, which is usually for rental purposes, we then begin the process of determining the 100% replacement value of the home.

I will contact the realtor to obtain a copy of the MLS listing for the property, which will give me the detailed information for that property. This information is very important to establish the 100% replacement for the property. We try very hard to provide insurance based on the replacement value.

After we have determined the amount of insurance to be written, I will call Hilda to advise the premium and she will let me know the closing date and who will hold the mortgage. I will receive a telephone call from the attorney's office handling the closing. The mortgage company will usually call to give me their "special wording" to be used for the mortgage clause. I will fax the Insurance Binder to both the attorney's office and the mortgage holder, mailing a copy to Hilda.

In the many years working with Hilda, I feel comfortable that the properties she is purchasing are, or will be in a reasonable time, in very good condition. If a property needs some cosmetic work, and some updating of either plumbing, heating or electrical systems, I know Hilda will take care of it.

She is a very conscientious property owner.

Maria Caprio
Vice-President
Starkweather and Shepley, Inc.
60 Catamore Boulevard
East Providence, Rhode Island 02914

Hilda Erfe, one of my grandest clients, is a great woman who truly lives life to the fullest-her cup is always half full. The enthusiasm and energy she exudes is reflected in the fun times she has on her trips, which leave her with pleasant and everlasting memories. As her travel agent for the past fifteen years, we have a great working and client relationship, with a feeling of being connected. Her friends and members of her family, even those out of state, return to me for their bookings. It is gratifying having quality clients like Hilda Erfe, who reflect loyalty and trust, particularly in this world of the internet. As a result, I feel she will be with me for many more years as she discovers new and exotic and interesting tours for her travels. In a nutshell, Hilda is my idol!

Charlene Haggarty
Destinations Travel
950 Wellington Avenue
Cranston, Rhode Island 02910

"The Smoking Gun" is a good description of this rather petite lady, but don't ever be fooled. She knows what she wants and will be patient till she gets it. Always on the go, she is always ready to respond to tenants. She has been most successful in all of her endeavors because I believe that she treats others as she would like to be treated. She is honest and just in all of her business transactions and loyal to those that deserve her loyalty.

In over twenty-three years of practicing real estate, I have met the one client that I also consider a dear friend.

Patsy Ewenson, GRI, CRS
Newport Rental Guide
(401) 848-8354

My essay on Hilda Erfe is more of a comical one. I every now and again remember what it was like to be a rental agent. I tend to focus on the negative instead of the positive. But in Hilda's case I always remember when she purchased 9 Cliff Terrace. Remember when I got those seven SWOS (Surface Warfare Officer's School) students. I remember being so concerned that she wouldn't close on time or that one of the students wouldn't graduate from the academy on time. But the funniest part was trying to describe the house to seven people who would be renting it without seeing it first. I remember thinking it would be perfect for seven women because of all of the flowery wallpaper. But, it turned out to be 6 guys and one girl...they all loved the wallpaper. I remember it fondly.

Kate Pomert
Newport Rental Guide
Newport, Rhode Island
(401) 848-8354

Working with Hilda Erfe has been a pleasure. Her properties are well-maintained at all times. She has handymen to deal with the problems of her many properties. If she is going to be out of town, she leaves the numbers with the tenants and we realtors where she can be reached at any time. She has chosen her handymen with great care. Knowing she has to count on them to get the job done without watching over them, especially if she is away.

As a landlord she treats her tenants with all due respect. She makes sure that they know this is their home for however long they are going to be there and what can she do to make it more comfortable for them. Not only does she make them totally comfortable with their home, she takes them and the realtor out to dinner to say thank you for choosing her property. What more can a tenant want?

As a realtor working for Hilda Erfe for the last eight years or longer, she has treated us with the utmost respect also. I can only wish that all landlords were like her! I personally have fourteen years experience and know what kind of tenants Hilda expects in her properties. I am not an agent that will just put anybody in her properties just for a commission. I would rather leave it vacant than to do that. I have an excellent rapport with her. There have been times when I would be away and have had a possible rental for her and she would do the showing and still pay me the commission. You try and find that with another landlord. If a problem should arise with any of my rentals that I have done for her, I will be the first to try and solve the problem, whether it be late rent or noisy tenants. I will definitely give them the tenants a call and give them my wrath! I am pretty good at "nipping it in the bud" before it escalates.

One cannot say one bad thing about her. She is the best landlord!

Loretta Restivo
Century 21, Access America
(401) 965-4000 / (800) 521-3336 x229

The hackneyed term "handyman" probably best describes my role in supporting Hilda's ownership and management of her rental properties. A variety of skills are required to respond to the unending series of routine and emergency tasks that need attention.

My observation is that rental property, whether it is vehicles, tools and appliances, or motels, hotels or residences receives a lot of "hard miles." Tenants seem to think that lack of ownership translates into little or no responsibility or respect is appropriate toward someone else's property.

This prevailing attitude, particularly towards short-term property results in a massive amount of replacing or repairing virtually everything, with which the tenant comes into contact. Part of my responsibilities are not only to actually salvage those items that have prematurely met their demise, but to observe and anticipate the vulnerability of them and to prepare for or minimize their frequent harsh treatment. For example, Hilda had difficulty in preventing tenants from damaging walls when they insisted on personalizing their bedrooms by fastening pictures and other objet d'art to their surfaces. Hilda's property has been traditionally rented on a short-term basis (three to six months), and creating holes in walls that require spackling and repainting on that repetitive basis is costly. Her refreshing and very effective idea is to protect wall surfaces by having me hang prints on the walls, so that tenants will not consider mounting their own artwork.

Hilda's sensitivity to tenants needs and concerns is unique and truly amazing. They are requested to make a list when they take occupancy of those items that they feel are missing, require attention or are inadequate. All reasonable requests are met with a favorable response.

Notification of tenants prior to maintenance and repairs is proper and considerate protocol, and also provides a basis for efficient scheduling of work. For example, showing up unannounced to repair a kitchen table at lunchtime as the tenants are preparing to eat would not be well received.

However, even with the best of planning and sensitive considerations and protocol, things can go awry. The following story occurred after Hilda had informed tenants that I would stop and check the integrity of the box springs and bed frames prior to their imminent departure and the soon-to-arrive new occupants.

It seems that beds receive especially “hard miles.” One can only speculate as to their cause of failure, such as Olympiad trampoline team members practicing in their bedrooms. Step one was to ring the front door bell twice and wait for a response. Step two was to insert a key and open the door and announce loudly and clearly who I was and why I was entering their apartment. In this particular case, I had to announce my presence twice before a tenant lumbered down the stairs to check on who I was. I informed the tenant of my mission and asked if anyone was upstairs in the bedrooms. He replied, “no, they’ve all left for the day.”

Most tenants do not make their beds before leaving in the morning so I was not surprised to see sheets, blankets, and pillows in complete disarray all across the bed tops. The procedure to check a bed foundation is to kneel at the foot of the bed, bend down and grab the left leg and shake the bed and then grab the right leg and shake the bed to see if it’s reasonably stable. Then I crawl around to one side of the bed and look at the connecting components of the bed frame to see if they are properly attached and look at the underside of the box spring to check for apparent or imminent failure. The beds in the three second floor bedrooms were judged to be okay. Being very focused on my mission I entered a third floor bedroom and immediately followed the usual integrity procedure.

After I checked the bed frame components and scanned the underside of the box spring, I began to raise my head above the top of the mattress, when much to my horror and embarrassment I viewed a hairy arm coming up from under a pile of sheets and blankets. Of course I immediately and profusely apologized for the intrusion, but the awakening tenant didn’t seem distressed about it at all. He said, “no problem man” as I sheepishly oozed out of the bedroom.

Ken Roberts
Maintenance Personnel

In the past few years, we here at Coristine Locksmith have been a great service to Hilda Erfe in her real estate business, doing service and calls and making keys. It has been a pleasure knowing her.

Hilda's responsibilities as a landlord require the majority of her time to be spent dealing with the public. Her outgoing personality and enthusiasm has created a pleasant relationship with us here at Coristine Locksmith.

Hilda has always displayed loyalty, honesty, and compassion and is an all-around pleasant person to be associated with. She is truly an asset to the real estate business and to us.

Lydia Gonzalez
Coristine Locksmith
Newport, Rhode Island

I would have to say that Mrs. Hilda Erfe is one of my most promising and caring customers. Hilda's bill is mailed out once a month and I can always count on her to pay on time. Our communication level is higher than any other customers I have.

I enjoy working for Mrs. Erfe. She is so kind. When I cut the lawns of Hilda's houses, I do it with precision. It has been a pleasure working for her and I hope to continue working with Hilda long into the future.

Roger Laodenio
Laodenio's Lawn Care
Middletown, Rhode Island

I have taken care of Mrs. Erfe on several occasions. I represent a neighborhood convenience hardware associated with Ace Hardware. We have generally supplied miscellaneous supplies directly to the rental properties or to persons in her employ. These include trash barrels (labeled with street address in marker pen) ice melt, snow shovels, rakes and cleaning supplies.

My comments are two, one for either side of the purchase transaction. First, we are a relatively small, independently owned and operated business with access primarily with the Ace cooperative but also other regional distributors. What that means is that we can usually fulfill a customer's needs within a few days if it is a large or unusual order; otherwise, we will probably have the product in stock that day. Although the business has primarily been build around Pittsburgh paints, there has always been a hardware side to it, which has grown with our recent expansion. Because of our size and our neighborhood location, we aggressively focus our service to all customers regardless of their size. Special orders are treated as just that. Customers are contacted when a special order comes in as well as when there might be a delay in delivery or some other unforeseen circumstance. Although in many instances we cannot compete with pricing found in the big stores, we do respectfully try to deliver value through our convenience and service as well as our pricing.

My second comment reflects the other side of the transaction, the customer. Mrs. Erfe has always been an upbeat, pleasant and direct person to work with. She usually knows what kind of product she is looking for, how much is reasonable to pay for it and any special requests she may have (such as labeling street addresses on the trash barrels.) All this is discussed up front before the transaction is completed. She receives a discount from us for purchases of volume as well as her account she has with us in the store. At the same time, she never 'nickel and dimes' the transaction to death. If she makes an appointment, she keeps it. Finally, she has established a sense of confidence and trust with us, hopefully one we have earned. I remember once there was a choice to be made regarding some snow shovels. She valued my judgment enough to ask me to make the decision. It is very gratifying to have a customer treat you with that regard. Although our transactions have probably not been sizeable in many respects, she thought enough to remember us at with gift certificates at Christmas, totally unexpected and uncalled for—but certainly appreciated.

Greg Dawson
Sales Associate
Richardson's Beach Hardware
58 Aquidneck Avenue
Middletown, Rhode Island 02840

My name is Malinda Shea and I run and own a gardening and landscape business called Malinda's Natural Designs. I first met Hilda in late spring of 2001. She owns and manages quite a few houses in Newport and she wanted me to put flower boxes and planters at her houses to make them more enjoyable to her guests. Designing and planting the boxes was no problem, but I explained to Hilda that maintaining and watering them would be very expensive. Most people do not want to pay a weekly fee to care for the flowers. I was surprised to find that Hilda did not hesitate, because she cared about her houses looking and feeling like home. Flowers and gardens add so much to a property, and Hilda knows and understands this.

When I agreed to do the job, she trusted me completely. I had free range in designing all of the boxes and planters. When she arrived home from a vacation and saw all of the houses we worked on, she was so excited and happy. It was so great to have such positive comments; she appreciated everything that we had done.

While working at the houses, we of course met most of the people who rent from Hilda. Everyone had nothing but praise for her. Time and time again, I kept hearing the same words about Hilda, "She really cares about her houses and the people who rent from her".

I am very busy these days, and really did not want to work on so many small places. Once I met Hilda, I could not say no to her! She has a presence about her that you can feel as soon as you meet her. Hilda is a very smart and strong woman, whose honesty and goodness shines from her.

I feel very lucky to know and work with Hilda. I hope to continue to do so in the future, she is a wonderful person. How you treat other people in life matters the most, and I believe that all you do will come back to you. Hilda will be blessed by her own kindness to others for the rest of her life.

Malinda Shea
Malinda's Natural Designs
Gardening and Landscape Business

I met Hilda through my father-in-law, Bill Connerton. She was looking for a maintenance person, and we hit it off right away. Hilda is a very high-energy go-getter. Every day is a learning experience for her. She is very safety-oriented, addresses problems aggressively and never takes no for an answer.

I've observed her in different environments. She knows when to talk and when to listen. In the short time we have known each other, she set the standards very high and wants everyone around her to do the same. The difference with Hilda is that she does this by example, and with a big heart and a happy attitude. In the seventeen years that I have been doing maintenance in private homes, condominiums and rental properties, I have never met a property manager who gives so much to the renters, workers and agents as she does. I believe the reason is because she is a genuine, caring person and the properties that she manages are hers.

Ed Coleman
General Maintenance and Painting
Newport, Rhode Island

I lived at 10 Champlain Street in Newport, Rhode Island, while I was attending Surface Warfare Officer School Division Officer Course from July 1997 through November 1997. You have been a wonderful landlady. You are friendly, extremely warm, supportive and especially understanding. I really appreciate how calmly you accepted my financial problem, and allowed me to pay my rent two weeks late. I doubt that anyone else would be so kind. You have been tremendously supportive throughout my life. I had a great time when you treated me for dinner when I was in Newport for a month and a half in January of 2000. When my ship, USS WASP (LHD 1) visited Boston, I made sure that you knew we were coming up. I thoroughly enjoyed giving you and your lovely friends a tour of my ship and later having lunch with you. Again you have been a wonderful landlady, mentor and friend. Hopefully when I come back to Newport for six months in August of 2003, I will rent a two-bedroom from Hilda! Thanks again.

Motale Efimba
US Navy Officer

My name is Jason Schwarzkopf, USNA class of 1997 and currently Navigator aboard USS Higgins DDG-76 stationed in San Diego, California. Prior to this tour, I was home ported in Sasebo, Japan and served as second division office onboard USS Germantown LSD-42. During that tour, I visited Hilda Erfe at her home in Cavite, just outside of Manila. I lived in one of her houses while in Newport and greatly enjoyed the camaraderie and great times in such a big house!

That house is ideal for a group of junior officers with five bedrooms, a full basement and garage for storage of biking, camping, dive gear and whatnot. During the summer and fall, we hosted many a party complete with barbecue, music and plenty of room on the front porch for dancing, socializing or just sitting and talking. For myself, and three fellow JO's, it became a home.

The turn-of-the-century style of the house includes a fireplace in the downstairs and vintage hardwood floors, which gives the place at truly comfortable atmosphere. What makes living here even more enjoyable is Hilda's other property next door-another five bedroom house! During my stay, both houses were home to four junior officers, and we all spent time planning parties or helping each other through school. The centralized location of this street means you are within walking distance of the waterfront and allows for easy navigation for anyone coming to visit.

I plan on attending department head school sometime in 2005, and would be happy to rent from Hilda again.

Jason Schwarzkopf
US Navy Officer

Second Letter from Jason Schwarzkopf following a visit to The Philippines

Thank you, Hilda, for the wonderful hospitality. Everyone appreciated all you did. They all loved the factory and the view of the volcano. The next day we just went shopping, but Thad was an incredible help. We are heading back to Okinawa now: thanks again for everything.

Jason Schwarzkopf
US Navy Officer

I just want to say that it was a pleasure staying at Hilda's house. I have given her number to the people who are coming to Newport next May, so she can expect a call if the houses have not already been leased.

James Rzonca
US Navy Officer

Jules Sherwood here out in Hawaii. I have returned from my deployment in the Pacific Ocean. We visited Guam, Japan, Thailand, South Korea, Palau, Phen Pei, Truk, Australia, Tonga and the Philippines. Unfortunately we were not allowed to leave the ship while in Manila, but thank you very much for such generous offers of hospitality!

I am moving again in Hawaii and was hoping I could use Hilda as a reference for my future landlord to contact.

Jules Sherwood
US Navy Officer

My stay in Newport has been wonderful. Since I had been separated from my husband for almost a year, being together as a family was very important to us. We found many things in Newport that were family friendly. The neighborhood welcomed us and was there to help out when needed. I felt like I had family all around me, even tough our extended families were far away.

My greatest joy has been renting our house. I fell in love with this house the moment I walked in the door. Even though we would only be here seven months, I knew this was a place I could call home. It was very well maintained, nicely decorated and furnished with all the necessary amenities. I felt immediately that the owner cared for us and made every effort to help us feel at home. After visiting the children and even our dog, I felt like we were partners with the same interest: keeping the utility costs down and preserving the natural beauty of the house. Because of the wonderful rapport I had with Hilda, I took great joy in going the extra mile to take care of the house or to plant flowers in the garden. I will leave here with a sad heart, but I will always remember the special friendship we developed.

Marge Sisco
Wife of USN Eric Sisco

Hilda, I cannot thank you enough for all you did for us while staying here at the house. For the nice dinner at Batik Garden, the prompt repair of the dishwasher and for simply being so gracious. We all enjoyed staying here and I was impressed by how well the house is kept up, including the yard work. The house provided everything we needed (dishes, furniture, washer and dryer, and hot water was never a problem.)

Chad Wedel
US Navy Officer

I just wanted to say thank you so much for your attention and service while we were living in 53 Hammond this year. It was very refreshing to have a landlord who took the time to meet us all and who was very, very quick to correct any discrepancies that came up. Dave, James, Eric and I truly enjoyed our time there, and a lot of that was due to the great relationship we had with you. I know that I, for one, will definitely recommend you to my fellow Navy friends if they are in Newport and I will look you up if I am ever in Newport again.

Once again, let me thank you for a truly enjoyable stay and I wish you all the best in the years to come.

Lee Donaldson
US Navy Officer

I lived at 415 Broadway. I needed a place to stay before leaving SWOS and Hilda's place was available. It is fully furnished with new appliances and ample room. The location is great since it is only five minutes from the base and downtown Newport.

Hilda is a great landlord who makes sure everything is in order. She is very easy to get in touch with and responds to our needs if something in the house has to be fixed. My stay there has been the most enjoyable out of all the places I have lived in Newport.

Suzanne Sclafani
US Navy Officer

Hilda, thank you for being the best landlady I have ever had. Your hospitality and warm visits remind me of my own home. If I'm ever in Newport, Rhode Island, I will make sure to give you a call. I will also refer future tenants to you!

Dennis Villena
US Navy Officer

Hilda, thanks for being a great landlord! The house was great and I really enjoyed my time while I was there. If I meet any Navy guys heading to Newport I will give them your name, thank you again.

David Groseclose, Christopher
McLain, Casey Tyree
US Navy Officers

I greatly enjoyed my stay at 20 Narragansett. It was an adorable little house and was perfect for my friends and I. It was our first year off campus and we were worried that we would not be able to find a place in the amount of time that we had. We were thrilled when we were shown this house and knew that it was the place for us.

The size of the house was just right. It was a small house but with just enough room for the three of us. We had a wonderful year there, with so many memories. I feel very lucky that we were able to live in this house and have such a great landlord, who was very willing to help us with anything that we needed.

Jennifer Kelly
Wilbraham, MA
Salve Regina University Student

We were never planning to live off campus. We did not think we could afford it. Then Salve notified us in December of our junior year that seniors and juniors would no longer be given housing unless there was a valid reason why they needed to stay on campus. We decided we had better start looking for an apartment since we knew that most people started earlier and so the best was probably already taken. We called the first realtor we thought of, which was DeWolfe. We needed something close to campus because we were not sure if we would all have cars or not. The realtor told us that she knew the perfect house for us, which was 20 Narragansett Avenue. We saw it one time before moving in August. Even though at the time there were messy guys living there, we fell in love with the place and we could envision our stuff in place of theirs.

It took us about a week to set the house up the way we wanted. We each had our own room for the first time while going to college. We had plenty of space for all of our belongings. Being girls we tended to bring way more than the necessities with us, and this time what did not fit in our rooms we could store in closets or other rooms in the house. The other highlight was the ability to cook our own meals. We no longer had to starve because we could not stomach the stuff the cafeteria called food. The kitchen was perfectly arranged and all the appliances worked well. We did not expect as much as was in the kitchen when we got there. Appliances like a dishwasher, microwave, toaster, and coffee makers we all added plusses that helped make our senior year of cooking even better.

At first it seemed unbelievable that we were living in a house. It was so wonderful and we did not have to worry about anything which was nice because we had a hard enough time figuring out who owed what for the food, phone and cable bills. The electricity and oil was included with a cap whatever we were over plus the water bill came out of our security deposit so we were worry-free. That was the highlight of living in the house. Since we were still going to school and also doing internships since we were seniors, it was nice not to have to worry about so many bills.

The house was in a nice neighborhood and we were able to chat with our neighbors when we saw them outside. We were not afraid of any crimes being committed and we felt safe. We felt comfortable and we took away many great memories from the house. We never had to worry about anything breaking because everything was well kept so we were free to make our last year of college a fun one—after we were done our homework! We took many great memories away of lounging on the couches every Thursday night to watch ER, sitting on the front porch in the fall evenings or the warm spring days, reading in the backyard, experimenting with new recipes in the kitchen, and having our own personal space in our bedrooms. We came to think of the house as our own and that made the experience so much better.

Hilda runs a wonderful management and we were very happy with the house. We could not have asked for better.

Jennifer Lamson
Lisbon, Maine
Elementary School Teacher

Seasons Greeting and Best Wishes for a Happy New Year.

Thanks very much for the hospitality and assistance you have given me.

Lt. Col. Zulkipli Sanni-Commanding Officer
3rd Bn. Royal Ranger Regiment
Oya Camp
Sibu, Sarawak, Malaysia
Foreign Sponsor

Special Thank You's:

There are some very special Navy officers who deserve recognition:

— Jason Schwarzkopf and Motale Efimba deserve a big hand for giving me a tour of their ships, USS Germantown in the Philippines and USS Wasp in Boston respectively.

— In 2001, Jennie Stone, Martha Katherine Macleod, Stephen Manzo, Jared Paul Belliveau, and Erin Durnan invited me to dinner at their home. They cooked sweet and sour chicken with rice. It was very good. I brought an apple pie from Gregg's restaurant, the best in Rhode Island!

— In 1996, Douglas Munz, Dean Wakeham, James Mill and Damon Dixon invited my husband Albert and I, and their realtor Helga Ganger to their home for a Chicken Cordon Bleu dinner with fresh salad. Helga brought the wine, I brought a pinwheel cheesecake and apple pie from Gregg's Restaurant. This group of men also belonged to the water polo and football teams.

— Joe Casale and Motale Efimba came back to Newport to take some additional courses, and we had dinner together.

—A big thank you to Joe Casale for referring four Navy Officer friends, namely Griffin Van Black, Donald Murphy, Dennis Villena and Ray Briggs.

—Another kudos for Michael Stoker and Mike Conrady for referring another Naval officer, Phil Hochgesang.

—A big 'thank you' for the wedding invitations from Jason Schwarzkopf and Dennis Villena. When I learn any of my tenants are getting married, I will usually give a gift before they leave, or I will mail it.

—A beautiful card from Motale Efima. I framed it and it hangs in the house. This was very thoughtful and appreciative.

There are Some Summer Tenants Who Deserve Recognition:

—John S. Dalsheim has rented the house by the water for the last five years, ever since I bought the property. He is the best. He has never missed holiday greetings each year. He gave me a book about Newport that my husband displays in our living room. He is always appreciative when I do some little favor for his group. He works for Janney, Montgomery and Scott, an investment brokerage firm in New York City. He has repeatedly invited me to have dinner with him when I visit The Big Apple.

He loved the flower boxes that Malinda put in the house. I make sure that I keep the same telephone number in that house for the summer. When I go home to the Philippines, I will bring him some Philippine cigars.

—Lee Potter and Fred Stanton have also rented the house along with John.

—Another group that has come to Newport and rented a house from me for the last two consecutive years, are Nicholas Van Taylor II, Eleanor Steward, Maurice Curran, and Matt Emans, Christopher Ruth, Brian Owens, and Dennis Campbell Mcrary. They hire someone to clean the house. I have never had any problems with them. They come to visit and enjoy Newport.

—The group of Steve Connolly, Jim Davis, Bill Davis, and Jim Cassidy has rented one of my houses since the mid 1990's. Now Steve's sister Kristin Connolly rents the house along with her group, John McDonald, Jennifer Eames and Jennifer Lucey. They have taken over the rental since the summer of 2000. I enjoy having them as tenants. They are all very nice, and quiet and just enjoy being in Newport for the summer. I think Steve's group are all married now.

Building Relationships Around Me

I would like to also say a very special and heartfelt thank you to the following people who have helped me over the years, and made my job as a landlord a lot easier and very enjoyable!

Accountants

Richard Hoopis was my accountant when I started buying the houses. I did everything by hand and I was very systematic. He left for Chicago to pursue another company.

I asked Dina, who was a Computer Science student, to help me with learning the computer.

I asked my friends for referrals to accountants. I interviewed a few of them until I felt at ease with one of them.

Dr. Basilia Ramirez recommended Ed Restivo as an accountant. My account is assigned to Helder Medeiros and Brian Frenett, the computer instructor. Helder and Brian must be accustomed to my surprises!

Merrill Lynch

I was with Merrill Lynch for over twenty-five years. Eugene Simone, my account executive and Marilyn Carroll, an administrative assistant, helped me all these years in buying stocks, getting mortgages and assisting me with the deposits when I go on vacation. They bend over backwards to make my life easier. The cashier ladies, especially Jannett, always have a smile and are ready to help. Dana greets me warmly as soon as I open the door. In turn, I bring them flowers from our garden during the summer.

Fidelity Investments

In the early 1990's, the money I saved was invested with Fidelity Investments. The money that I made from the investments was used to for repairs and upgrades on some of my houses. My account executives were Carroll William Hayes, Chris Fahey, who left Fidelity, and currently I work with Jim Capra from the Braintree branch.

First Federal Bank

My accountant, Helder Medeiros, recommended First Federal Savings Bank of America to give me one of the LLC's, a "fund capital improvements to investment property".

Mr. Douglas F. Hanson, Vice-President Business Bank of First Federal handled all of the transactions. It took less than four weeks for completion. John Garrahy, lawyer for the bank, prepared the documents. Knud Hellested, manager of the downtown office along with Meredith Gibson have all helped me with the accounts.

Lamoriello and Company

Anna Guilmette from Lamoriello and Company our plan administrator, did the research on real estate provisions in the pension plan.

GMAC

For almost ten years, GMAC Mortgage Company has been providing mortgages for the houses. GMAC has different programs to suit what I need, according to Lynn LaFontaine my mortgage coordinator.

About two years ago, I was flying to the Philippines on Northwest Airlines. I read in the Northwest Airlines Magazine, that GMAC is a partner of Northwest Airlines. I could earn frequent flyer miles by buying or refinancing a house through GMAC. I contacted them as soon as I purchased another house. Since that time I have bought three houses and refinanced three times. I still have not seen any mileage in my account.

Lawyer

My mortgage company, GMAC, uses John McGreen of Taft and McSally law firm as their lawyer. After I had closed on several properties, I have gotten to know Mr. McGreen quite well. I utilize his expertise in all areas of real estate legal issues including going to court, tenant violations and obtaining the other necessary paperwork for the houses and my husband's office.

Mr. John Harpootian, my trust lawyer, did a simplified and trust document so that I could easily understand the wording.

Allstates 1031 X-Change Facilitator, LLC (www.allstates1031.com)

My accountant recommended F. Moore McLaughlin, an attorney, to process the 1031 Exchange as the Qualified Intermediary.

Paul J. DeLuise, CPA, is the President of Allstates and was kind enough to send me all of the information I have provided in a previous chapter. Allstates conducts seminars all over the country. Their main offices are in Boston, Massachusetts and Providence, Rhode Island.

Insurance company

Maria Caprio from Starkweather and Sheply Insurance Brokerage, Inc. from Providence is my insurance agent. She is always available when I need her!

Real Estate Company

A few times a year, I will ask Ed Kedzierski from Newport Rental Guide to give me a market analysis of my houses to check for their appreciation. This is very important in the strategy of my business.

I have a very good and energetic relationship with all of the realtors!

Realtors

Here is a list of realtors that I always use for business:

Newport Rental Guide		(800) 972-5169	Kate x 162
	Patsy x159	Kelly x 250	MaryEllen x255
	Annabelle x 263	Amy x 251	Ann x 154
Century 21-Access America			
	Loretta Restivo	(800) 521-3336 x229	
		(401) 965-4000	
	Beverly Black	(401) 935-2224	
	Dotty Herwin	(401) 855-1735	
	Jeannie Allen	(401) 849-9192	
Bellevue Realtor		(401) 849-6084	
	Ellen Miller x 127	or	
		(401) 255-6151	
	Barbara, John,	Tracy	
ReMax:			
	Edith Cushing	(401) 848-6750	
	Kate Winthrop	(401) 835-0177	
Osborn Realty:		(401) 849-4150	
	Jim Osborn		
Capitol Realty:		(401) 849-4220	
	Suzie, Joann,	Ronnie,	Veronica, Marty

Lila Delman Realty (401) 848-2101
Louise Cardoni

Island Rentals: (800) 827-5717
Christine Gignere

America's Realty: (800) 314-6673
Diane McLeod, Shelly Mathes

Prudential Realty: (401) 849-1800
Vickie Little (401) 855-8080
JoEllen (401) 261-3777

Private Properties: (401) 846-9000
Peter, Barbara, Roslyn

Hogan and Stone: (401) 849-6700
Chad Kritzas, Sharon Foster, Collin Kelly
Joe, Sherryl

Heritage of Newport: (800) 343-9323
Ann, Ruth

Carey Richmond: (401) 848-6659
Donna Lunney (401) 848-6605

Century 21 Boulevard: (401) 842-6900
Megan, Cheryl

HILDA'S HINT

Run after the realtor who gives you bad and noisy tenants. Tell the realtor that they need to take care of fixing the problems with these tenants! The realtors that I have listed above are the absolute very best!

New York City Realtors:

Fox Residential Group:
(212) 772-2666
Gloria Sokolin,
Angela Latigona

William B. May Realty Company:
(212) 829-8000
Shlomo Manne

The Corcoran Group:
(212) 355-3550
Richelle Spindell

City Hall

Mr. Dermot McDermott is the meter supervisor for the water department. Mary Scott is the municipal court clerk along with Debra Vingadannis. Linda Williams, Joan Gourgas and Kim Collins are in the registration department.

Allan Booth is the tax assessor. Joseph Crowshaw is Newport's tax collector. Michael J. Coury is the Human Resource Administrator. Office Patrick Shea, community police officer, and Ed Coleman (my maintenance associate as well as local fireman) took care of the tenant's noise complaint. I commend the people of City Hall for all of their hard work!

However, there is only one employee at City Hall that hates my guts! The hate was so strong that I could sense it! When I first started buying the houses and dealing with City Hall for various things, I often went to this employee's office to get some advice. He treated me like I was a statue standing there. He always had a blank look on his face and would not utter a word. Up to this time, the employee held a grudge against me. Recently, I was sited again. I told the realtor to fix the problem with the tenants. I told her to go around the neighborhood and give out her business cards. Well, my realtor left a message for the City Hall employee, telling him that she straightened out the problem tenants. I was *very upset* when this employee returned the message that he did not utter a single word to the realtor, except to tell her that I have a history of 'party houses.' I have worked long and hard to solve these problems, and I have selected a good realtor who really cares about me. I have not been into court for a long time. Even the judge commented to my attorney that he had been away for quite a while. Everyone asks me why this employee hates me. I tell them that this is the way he has been since I have been buying houses in Newport. He should not be employed at City Hall if he cannot be fair. The Mayor and the business manager should straighten him out! I usually stay away from him, and bring my problems to my attorney. It is very sad, he should realize that I pay taxes in Newport and I contribute to his paycheck.

Michael Mallinoff, the business manager, and Joseph Nicholson, Jr., the solicitor, were the ones who gave me the pointers on how to solve the noise problems. I thank them for their never-ending help.

Mayor Richard C. Sardella of Newport, Rhode Island was kind enough to give me a contribution for my book. The secretary of the Mayor, Dorothy Baccari, was also very accommodating.

Maintenance Personnel

A retired Navy man, Frank Britto was one of my first maintenance people. He is one person that I deeply respect. He will always protect the business. He will show me why the house is not solid. He is always right.

By the time I bought by seventh house, I was established and knew how to select good people to work with me. I got Chris Electric, Boulevard Plumbing, RJ Cawley Construction, Baystate Flooring, Loadenio's Lawn Care and Movers, Richardson's Beach Hardware, Dirty Harry Laundry Mat, Curtain Factory Outlet, William Connerton for fire safety, Sherwin Williams Paints, Newport Gutters, Ken Roberts, Gina Delgado, Ed Coleman, Gregg Dawson, Milton and Tiana Cardoso, Judy Canlas, Linda & Raul Gutierrez, Tony Gonsalves and many others.

Ken Roberts, a retired engineer from Raytheon, decided he could not stay home after retirement. He needed something to keep him busy. He can do anything, including painting. Ken is in charge of hanging the pictures in all the houses. He is the only one I trust with this matter. He measures the distance and he makes sure that the picture is center or proportional to the walls, and always checks for the stud. He is an excellent painter and neatly cleans up after he is finished He also hangs the hardware for the curtains and as well as all of the mini-blinds. He is an expert in changing window ropes. Anything he does is very precise! Ken also took courses at MIT and sometimes we talk like "techies" when we do projects together at the house.

One day I was outside in front of House #1 and as I was getting ready to leave. I saw Bill Connerton coming out of his house with a piece of paper in his hand. I opened my window and he asked me if I had any painting jobs for his son-in-law, Ed Coleman, a good painter. I got Ed's phone number, and the next day left a message on his answering machine. I wanted to know when he was free to do some painting, as we had a problem at the condominium. The bathroom on the second floor had water leaking through the ceiling to the dining room on the first floor. The paints were peeling and were scattered all over the floor. That was his first job. He said he could also do a lot of other things around the house. He is now hooked in the houses. He is a very good maintenance person. When the tenants ask him to fix a toilet, the toilet is fixed and I do not receive a second call from the tenants. This is my basis of telling if the maintenance man is any good.

Lawn care is as important as anything you have to do around the house. It gives everyone a first impression when looking at your house. Roger Loadenio is our maintenance landscaper and also has a truck therefore he does all of the furniture moving from house to house. He also throws out big garbage or takes junk to the dump. He will pick up furniture or anything that cannot fit my car. I also deal with another landscaping company, Little Landscaping. They are very helpful as well.

Message from Hilda

I sent e-mails to one of my maintenance people when I felt he was not focusing one hundred percent on his job. Here is an excerpt of that e-mail:

"When I ask someone to work for me, I will observe that person for a few months. I have to learn their views, how they work, how they take their assignments, how they go about finishing the job. I will know if they run around trying to do their other work and they are not accomplishing my assignment.

When I give my other maintenance personnel an assignment, they surpass my expectations and do excellent work. I do not have to supervise them. They are very responsible.

All of them are conscientious of the expenses that go in this kind of business. If they think that they can save me some money, they will not hesitate to tell or remind me and suggest ways to save."

HILDA

I will only write or e-mail a maintenance person if he is a good, efficient, and widely knowledgeable worker, to give him advice. I always give a second chance. I have trained many people, and you can spot right away someone who cannot focus. I do not usually ask anyone to supervise the maintenance people. This job is small and it does not warranty a supervisor. I just do it myself.

The e-mail worked. This maintenance person is focused now. He already knows what I want in painting the interior of the house. Once the maintenance man knows what I want, I leave him alone to do their job.

Keys

After a year in buying houses, I went to a local locksmith and inquired if they could re-key one of the houses. He came to the house and my life now is so much easier. I then called him to question an invoice. His secretary did not like my questioning. After this incident, I called again and they gave me a song and dance saying that he was busy and was not available. My patience is now near rock bottom, because I still needed to find a way to handle all of these different keys without losing my mind! I finally called another locksmith in town, Coristine Locksmith. If I go into the store and Lydia is working she makes sure I get waited on immediately. These locksmiths are my saving grace. Mario, Gary, Kevin and Wayne are angels. When I call them, they come right away, do their job, and send me an invoice. They re-keyed all the houses and tagged them with numbers (if the house number is 32, that is what they embossed on the key). I now have only one ring of keys that are numerically arranged. This idea came from Ken Roberts, our maintenance personnel. They also saved me when I locked my keys in my car!

Windows

Sharon from Weatherseal Window Company installed all our new windows. Sharon has good, efficient and knowledgeable installers, Leo Benoit and Cory Atkins. They are neat and throw the old windows away. If the trim is rotten, they change it. They insulate the sides of the windows and caulk around the frames. After they install the windows they put the blinds and curtains back in their original place.

Attic

When I had a problem with the attic I called a carpenter, Dan Finnegan of Finnegan Construction, who was recommended to me by my neighbor, Pauline Shea. Dan inspected the hole in the attic and eventually repaired it to avoid the same problem from happening again.

Landscaping

Roger Laodenio is my landscaper. He does a beautiful job with the lawns and keeps the hedges trimmed as well. I have another person, Johnnie Shea, who maintains the hedges on one of the houses. Rudy and Ruding Parayno (twin brothers originally from the Philippines) assist with the lawns and also help to move the furniture.

Another landscaping company I am currently using is Little Landscaping. Jerry, Alan and Richard work there. Their mother, Terry, helps her sons manage the business.

Porch

John from One Stop Builders showed me Cabot stain, when I told him about the bleeding problem on the porch.

Roof

Leo Benoit from Weatherseal who was installing some windows, noticed that the roof over the porch was sagging. This was an emergency, so I had Ken Roberts support the roof before I can get estimates for the repair.

Jim Facer from of Quality Exterior of Warwick, Rhode Island, did the roof at the other house with asbestos roofing. Rather than fix or repair it, I decided to remove the asbestos and install asphalt shingles.

Dan Finnegan did the roof at the other house. He repaired the roof and the rotten wood gutters.

Flower Boxes

I asked around at the flower garden shop if they knew anybody who can do flower boxes. Finally I met Gregg Dawson from Richardson Beach and Hardware while I was buying some impatiens flowers, and I asked him if he knew anyone who would be able to handle this for me. Gregg immediately went to work on this project. He recommended Malinda from Malinda's Natural Flower Design.

Plumbing

David Denyo of Boulevard Plumbing is one of my plumbers who I can trust. I also call Roto-Rooter frequently. Edwin Maldonado, John Gutierrez and Charlotte Laiter handle the job from Roto-Rooter.

Heater, Boiler, Water Heater

I found that Reliable Oil does the best service.

Their customer service agents Kathy (retired) Sue, Wendy, Tracy, Bob, Ron, Wayne, and Debbie, are superb!

Air-Conditioning Units

John Cedeno from Rhode Island Mechanical Service, Inc. maintains the heating and air-condition. A new air conditioning company that I have been using is HV Holland, from Jamestown, Rhode Island. They are very nice and efficient.

Telephone and Cable

Ken Middleton is our telephone man. When I need him for service or repair, he comes immediately. It depends on the request of the tenants how many lines they need.

Pest Control

Griggs and Brown have maintained my personal home's pest control quarterly. I have used them for twenty-five years. I called David Hartley to take care of our houses in Newport. I have contracts with them.

Maintenance Cleaning

Gina Delgado, Milton and Tiana Cardoso, Judy Canlas do the interior cleaning of all my houses. If they cannot handle the cleaning workload, they will get help from friends and I will pay them separately. They have full time jobs, as our work is only busy during the summer. Some of their helpers are Elena, Marge, Linda and Raul.

Laundromat

Mary Steinhouse is in charge of Dirty Harry Laundromat.

Floors

I found Steve Bertoncini of Bay State Floor from Fall River, Massachusetts, who was recommended by Tony Gonsalves, another maintenance personnel. Steve and his group, Steve Fagan and Mark Perreira are excellent in their trade.

Interior Painting

My paint suppliers are Sherwin William, Richardson's Beach and Hardware (Pittsburgh Paints) and Benjamin Moore paints.

My painters are Ken Roberts, Gregg Dawson, Ed Coleman, Steve Kenneally and Ed Rose. They have their own artistic way of making the colors blend. I learned a lot from them. I always tell them to caulk. Otherwise the work will just go down in the drain! It bothers me to see an uncaulked wall, which make me nuts!

Appliances

Bill, Joe, Pam, Sharon and other service technicians from Sturm's Appliance are willing and able to assist me with any purchases or repairs.

Window Treatments

A friend, Connie Chamberland, showed me the Curtain Factory Outlet in Northbridge, Massachusetts. I met the manager, Kay, and asked her to help me pick up some curtains for one of the houses

Carpet

Randy, the owner of All Pro Carpet cleaning, steam cleans the carpet in the condominium and picks up the area rugs in the other houses to be cleaned. He takes them to his shop and delivers them after three to four days.

Furniture

When I was starting my business, I went to see Roger, from Roline

Furniture in Blackstone, Massachusetts, and I bought furnishings for all the houses.

Alpert's Furniture is my local furniture dealer. Joe Da Silva is my local salesman. He makes sure that I am taken care of with all of my furniture orders.

Wicker Chairs

Don Stone of Yankee Cane and Upholstery repaired the set of wicker furniture that was in the waterfront house. Valentin Freas works with Don Stone and is invaluable!

My Car

I purchased my fifth Subaru Imprezza from Bald Hill Subaru. I love my Subaru!!! The car is my second office. I am very particular on the maintenance for the car. I do not like to get stuck on the highway.

Gutters

Glen Cameron is my savior on gutters. He maintains and inspects the gutters once a year. I do not have to call him; he sets his schedule and bills me later.

Travel Agent

Charlene Haggarty of Destination Travel handles my plane, car and hotel reservations when I visit the out of state properties. She makes sure I get a good deal.

Suppliers

Richardson's Beach and Hardware is my supplier for general household items. They *deliver* which I love and need, because I have a small car. I buy paints and they keep a record of the colors that we need for each house. My maintenance person also gets his supplies from Newport Hardware.

Home Depot is another supplier where I can buy anything for construction that we need. I learn a lot just visiting their store. They also deliver!

One Stop Builders also offers same-day delivery! What more can you ask? They delivered a grill for the tenants to be used on Memorial Day weekend.

Lastly I would like to thank my friends, Phyliss Corrado and Elvie Danho, for keeping me company when I visit my houses in Newport and Hilton Head.

CHAPTER 12 Final Thoughts

"From the jagged coastline to the 'cottages' that line Bellevue Avenue, Newport continues to be America's First Resort. Over three and one half million people visit our City each year to marvel at the colonial architecture, enjoy the fine restaurants and shops, and relax at one of our many beaches. Whether you enjoy sailing Narragansett Bay or listening to world class music at the festivals, Newport has a unique blend of activities to offer."

— ***Richard C. Sardella***
Mayor, City of Newport, Rhode Island

My job as landlord would not be so enjoyable and fulfilling, without the beauty, historical significance and the wonderful people who live, work and vacation in the city of Newport, Rhode Island. It is a city with remarkable houses, and people who take pride in their work and in caring for their homes, and mine!

When I began to write this book, I thought I had only a few ideas in to put down on paper. As I went along gathering my thoughts and writing them down, I realized that I accomplished so much in these last few years. I enjoy the job, and the years pass without my noticing how much work I do. I treasure the friends that I have met, and the tenants, neighbors and business associates.

The success of this undertaking for me has to have the cooperation of my husband. He does not argue with me on investments. He is very busy and does not know where most of my houses are located. I gave him some tips on how I run my business, and ask that he answer the telephone politely, and write down my messages. Perhaps the most important advice I gave to him was that after he listens to the answering machine; please do not delete the messages!

In my book, I have laid out the basics of buying and renting houses. I have worked diligently on each task every day and solve problems as they arise. The most important thing to remember is to focus on the job. I have given thorough details of what must be done to succeed in real estate investing. Always think positive, even if everything seems like it is falling apart around you.

I hope that you have learned and picked up a few pointers from my experiences. Do not be afraid to start on this venture. Have guts. I usually do not announce my projects publicly when I start them, as I do not like to hear discouraging advice. Develop self-confidence and have a positive attitude.

First and foremost, I train myself. Every day I learn another lesson. I welcome lessons, which will give me progress and experience. Do not be shy when approaching the bank for financing. If you have to go to more than one lender to compare rates, that is fine.

Practice going to open houses and learn from the realtors how to buy a good rental property and what you should look for. You will not be bothering anyone if you make an appointment, and you will not get any pressure from the realtors.

When the maintenance people see that you are knowledgeable, they will treat you fairly. Do the necessary repairs to maintain the houses then you rent or sell. Have good relationships with everyone around you, and everything will fall right into place. Develop your own personal strategy and have good foresight. I always say that food is the best way to success! I enjoy treating my tenants, maintenance team and other vendors to pizza, Dunkin Donuts and Chinese food buffet!

Basic, Basic, Basic!! You can more or less learn how much a project will cost for repairing bathrooms, roofs, painting, cleaning, yard maintenance and the like. These simple basics will determine the structure on whether or not you may decide to buy a certain property.

HILDA'S RULES OF THUMB

- Do not be afraid to work.
- Think of work as fun!
- Location, Location, Location
- Start and maintain good working relationships.
- Keep your houses in good condition…always have them ready to rent or sell.
- Think positive, it helps to relieve stress.
- Go on vacation at least once or twice a year.
- If there is a problem, find a solution. Do not brood or sit on it.
- Do not expect to receive high rents, you will get stress.
- If there is a vacancy calm yourself, this is part of business. Set money aside for emergencies.
- If you have built equity into your property, apply for an equity loan if needed.
- I always meet and greet my tenants on moving day and welcome them. If the tenants are college students I will also meet their families. I provide tenants with notices of information including the telephone numbers of maintenance personnel, and I always try to memorize their names.

Appendix

Introductory Notice

Welcome to (*house address*)____________________________________!

Please note:

1. Anything that you remove from the house while you are a tenant must be returned to its original place at the end of the lease. For example: Curtains, pictures, beds, dressers, mirrors etc.

   If you must remove any item, please be sure that it is properly and safely stored away.

2. Decals on the ceiling and walls are not allowed.

3. Bill Connerton, the former Fire Chief of Newport, will be checking the fire alarms twice a year during daylight savings time. Please be cooperative.

4. The checkout time at the end of the lease is 11:00 am.

5. The Garbage Ordinance of Newport and the schedule is included in this package.

6. The house must be cleaned before you leave at the end of the lease. If the house is left dirty, you will be charged for the cleaning.

7. Salve Regina University will be notified of your tenancy and telephone number if you are a student. The Dean of Student Affairs will be given a copy.

Hilda Erfe
Phone: xxx-xxx-xxxx
Cell: xxx-xxx-xxxx
Fax: xxx-xxx-xxxx

Introductory Notice
Maintenance Personnel Information

Important Reminders:

- Please do not overload toilets with toilet paper.
- Sanitary napkins will clog the drains!
  (Charge for unclogging the toilet is $40.00).
- Neighbors and I will not tolerate loud music, loud noises or parties!

If I cannot be reached for a maintenance issue please call one of the following and state your problem:

Maintenance Persons:

Ed Coleman	xxx-xxxx or xxx-xxxx (cell phone)	
Little Landscaping	xxx-xxxx	*Lawn Maintenance and Cleaning*

With regard to the utilities, please call the following companies **before** you call the maintenance person. We have service contracts with these companies. **You need to mention: Hilda Erfe and house address.**

Sturm's Appliances	xxx-xxxx	*They service all of the appliances*
Reliable Oil	1-800-xxx-xxxx	*Problems concerning, heating, boiler, leaking radiator, water heater, etc. They have 24 hour service.*
Providence Gas	xxx-xxxx or 1-800 xxx-xxxx	*for Misty Harbor*
H.V. Holland	xxx-xxxx	*Air Conditioning for Misty Harbor*

Coristine Locksmith	xxx-xxxx	*If you lose your keys, call them or call your realtor. They have extra keys. Please do not kick or destroy the doors.*
Judy or Milton	xxx-xxxx	*Cleaning service* *Cleaning service fee is $12-15 per hour. Approximately $40 for a 2BR, $60 for a 5BR and $70 for a 7BR. Summer rental includes the entire house, porch and washing the linens and towels.*

Your Realtor can also help you if you cannot get in touch with any of these people.

Winter Notice

- **When leaving for the holidays, please leave your thermostat set at 68 degrees.**

- **Please close all storm windows and be sure that all windows and doors are locked.**

Merry Christmas and a very Happy New Year!!!

HILDA

Garbage Collection Information

Hilda Erfe
Phone: xxx-xxx-xxxx

Pickup:

House #1	Wednesday
House #2	Thursday
House #3	Monday
House #4	Thursday
House #5	Friday
House #6	Monday
House #7	Thursday

Tenant Violation Form

As noted in your lease agreement and discussed with you by your realtor and myself, the City of Newport has strict guidelines which must be followed. Please read carefully and sign this form and return it to me as soon as possible.

Zoning Enforcement and Garbage Ordinance:

Under Section 8.24 of the Codified Ordinance of the City of Newport, all household solid waste must be stored and set out to the curb for collection in barrels with tightly fitting, watertight lids. All bags containing garbage must be stored in a barrel at all times and are not to be placed curbside without being placed in a barrel. Areas where garbage barrels are stored and the containers themselves must be maintained in a nuisance-free, odor-free condition. Also note that the ordinance requires that all trash containers are to be placed curbside the night prior to or the morning of the pickup. All trash containers are to be removed the same day as the pickup. Residents setting out or storing garbage without the use of approved containers or storing containers in such a way as to create a nuisance will be subject to a fine of up to $500.00.

Tenants Names: ______________________________

____

____

____

Signatures of All Tenants: ______________________________

____

____

Address: ______________________________

____

Date ______________________________

Calendar

Hilda Erfe: xxx-xxxx

Ⓧ Denotes Occupied

January 2002

SUN	MON	TUE	WED	THR	FRI	SAT
		1	2	3	4	5
6	7	8	9	10	11	12
13	14	15	16	17	18	19
20	21	22	23	24	25	26
27	28	29	30	31		

April 2002

SUN	MON	TUE	WED	THR	FRI	SAT
9	1	2	3	4	5	6
7	8	9	10	11	12	13
14	15	16	17	18	19	20
21	22	23	24	25	26	27
28	29	30				

Clean

February 2002

SUN	MON	TUE	WED	THR	FRI	SAT
					1	2
3	4	5	6	7	8	9
10	11	12	13	14	15	16
17	18	19	20	21	22	23
24	25	26	27	28		

May 2002

Maintenance Repairs

SUN	MON	TUE	WED	THR	FRI	SAT
		1	1	2	3	4
5	6	7	8	9	10	11
12	13		15	16	17	18
19	20	21	22	23	24	25
26	27	28	29	30	31	

Check Linens

March 2002

SUN	MON	TUE	WED	THR	FRI	SAT
					1	2
3	4	5	6	7	8	9
10	11	12	13	14	15	16
17	18	19	20	21	22	23
24	25	26	27	28	29	30/31

June 2002

SUN	MON	TUE	WED	THR	FRI	SAT
						1
2	3	4	5	6	7	8
9	10	11	12	13	14	15
16	17	18	19	20	21	22
23/30						

Philippines Phone: xxx-xx-xx-xxx-xxxx

Best Time to call...U.S. Time 6 - 10 am **Vacation Month__________**

July 2002

SUN	MON	TUE	WED	THR	FRI	SAT
	1	2	3	4	5	6
7	8	9	10	11	12	13
14	15	16	17	18	19	20
21	22	23	24	25	26	27
28	29	30				

August 2002

SUN	MON	TUE	WED	THR	FRI	SAT
				1	2	3
4	5	6	7	8	9	10
11	12	13	14	15	16	17
18	19	20	21	22	23	24
25	26	27	28	29	30	31

September 2002

SUN	MON	TUE	WED	THR	FRI	SAT
1	2 Clean	3	4	5	6	7
8	9	10	11	12	13	14
15	16	17	18	19	20	21
22	23	24	25	26	27	28
29	30					

October 2002

SUN	MON	TUE	WED	THR	FRI	SAT
		1	2	3	4	5
6	7	8	9	10	11	12
13	14	15	16	17	18	19
20	21	22	23	24	25	26
27	28	29	30	31		

November 2002

SUN	MON	TUE	WED	THR	FRI	SAT
					1	2
3	4	5	6	7	8	9
10	11	12	13	14	15	16
17	18	19	20	21	22	23
24	25	26	27	28	29	30

December 2002

SUN	MON	TUE	WED	THR	FRI	SAT
1	2	3	4	5	6	7
8	9	10	11	12	13	14
15	16	17	18	19	20	21
22	23	24	25	26	27	28
29	30	31				

Mileage Chart

Date	Travel To	Mileage Start	Mileage End	Reason for Visit
7/15/02	Newport	45055	45100	Meet tenants at house

Excerpt from Investment Property Exchange Services, Inc./www.ipx1031.com.

The tax deferred exchange, as defined in Section 1031 of the Internal Revenue Code of 1986, as amended, offers real estate investors one of the last great investment opportunities to build wealth and save taxes. By completing an exchange, the investor (Exchanger) can dispose of their investment property, use all of the equity to acquire replacement investment property, defer the capital gain tax that would ordinarily be paid, and leverage all of their equity into the replacement property. Two requirements must be met to defer the capital gain tax: (a) the Exchanger must acquire "like kind" replacement property and (b) the Exchanger cannot receive cash or other benefits (unless the Exchanger pays capital gain taxes on this money.)

In any exchange, the Exchanger must enter into the exchange transaction prior to the close of the relinquished property. The Exchanger and the Qualified Intermediary enter into an Exchange Agreement, which essentially requires that (a) the Qualified Intermediary acquires the relinquished property from the Exchanger and transfers it to the buyer by a direct deed from the Exchanger and (b) the Qualified Intermediary acquires the replacement property from the seller and transfers it to the Exchanger by a direct deed from the seller. The cash or other proceeds from the relinquished property are assigned to the Qualified Intermediary, and are held by the Qualified Intermediary in a separate secure account. The exchange funds are used by the Qualified Intermediary to purchase the replacement property for the Exchanger.

Exchanges must be completed within strict time limits with absolutely no extensions. The Exchanger has forty-five days from the date the relinquished property closes to "Identify" potential replacement properties. This involves a written notification to the Qualified Intermediary listing the addresses or legal descriptions of the potential replacement properties. The purchase of the replacement property must be completed within one-hundred eighty days after of the close of the relinquished property. After the forty-five days has passed, the Exchanger may not change their Property Identification list and must purchase one of the listed replacement properties or the exchange fails!

Investment Property Exchange Services, Inc. is available to assist Exchangers and their advisors with their exchange strategies. **The Exchanger is always advised to discuss the intended exchange with their legal or tax advisor.**

Generally, investors complete tax-deferred exchanges to defer the capital gains tax on the disposition of their investment properties. However, there are many additional underlying reasons an investor might want to exchange one property for another. The motives often fall along standard risk—reward or cash flow—appreciation scales. These are some of the typical non-tax motives to exchange:

- Exchange from fully depreciated property to a higher value property that can be depreciated.

- Exchange from property, which cannot be refinanced, such as vacant land, to improved property, which will support a new loan, thereby giving the client the ability to obtain cash after the acquisition of the replacement property.

- Exchange from non-income producing raw land to improved property to create a cash flow from the rental income.

- Exchange from a property with maximized or minimal cash flow, such as an apartment building, to a higher cash flow property, such as a retail shopping center to generate a larger cash flow.

- Exchange from a stagnant or slowly appreciating property to a property in an area with faster appreciation.

- Exchange for a property or properties that may be easier to sell in the coming years.

- Exchange to meet the client's locational requirements, for example, the client moves to another state and wants to have their investment property nearby.

- Exchange to fit the lifestyle of a client, for example, a retiree may exchange for a property requiring reduced management responsibility so they can do more traveling.

- Exchange from several smaller properties to one larger property to consolidate the benefits of ownership and reduce management responsibilities.

- Exchange from a larger property to several smaller properties to divide an estate among several children or for retirement reasons.

- Exchange to a property the client can use in his or her own profession, for example a doctor may exchange from a rental house to a medical building to use for their practice.

- Exchange from a partial interest in one property to a full interest in another property.

- Exchange from a management intensive fee interest in real estate to a triple net leased property where the lease, including options, has 30 or more years remaining."

Excerpt from Allstates 1031 X-Change Facilitator, LLC (www.Allstates1031.com)

45-Day Identification of Replacement Property

"Under Regulations issued by the Internal Revenue Service for IRC 1031 tax-deferred exchanges, there are stringent requirements regarding identification of replacement property. These requirements must be met before the expiration of 45 days from the date you relinquished your exchange property.

Identification of all replacement property must be made in writing, must be signed by you, and must be delivered to us on or before the 45th day. You may not identify replacement property after the 45th day.

You may identify as many as three properties, regardless of their total value (the "3 property rule") or you may identify any number of properties provided their aggregate fair market value on the 45th day does not exceed 200% of the aggregate fair market value of all your relinquished property on the date of its transfer (the "200% rule"). If you stay within these rules, you do not need to acquire all the property you identified. There are serious consequences if you do not stay within either of these rules. We recommend that you follow the 3-property rule, and identify either two or three properties, so that if the closing on your preferred property fails for any reason, you will have made a timely identification of one or two alternate properties which may be acquired instead.

You may identify any type of investment or business property, single family rental, duplex, apartment building, hotel, office building, warehouse, commercial building, vacant land, etc.

You may identify property in any State of the United States. Your identification must be specific as to what you intend to purchase. For example, if you intend to purchase only a percentage interest in a piece of property, you must identify it as "_______% interest in ..." If you intend to construct improvements, you must describe specifically what improvements you intend to make, in addition to listing the address or legal description of the property where the improvements will be located. There are restrictions on acquiring property from related persons. If you plan to do so, please call us.

It is easy to identify the property to us after you have selected it. Simply write us a letter, using the form enclosed, giving either the street address or legal description of the property, stating that you identify it as replacement property. Sign the letter, and send it to us by mail or by fax, so that it reaches us by midnight on the 45th day.

Allstates 1031 has a newsletter at www.allstates1031.com. The exchanger is always advised to discuss the intended exchange with their legal council.

TO ORDER additional copies of *Real Estate 101 Buying - Real Estate 102 Renting* do the following:

For credit card orders, call toll free, Book Clearing House, **800-431-1579** *(24 hours a day, 7 days a week)*

You can also order through the website: **www.bookch.com** or send email to: **bookch@aol.com**

Or, return this order form with your check or money order to:

Book Clearing House
46 Purdy Street
Harrison, NY 10528

Make checks/money orders payable to "Book Clearing House."

Please complete the following information for shipping;

	Quantity		**Price**		**Total**
Real Estate 101 Buying – Real Estate 102 Renting	________	X	$19.95	=	$________
Rhode Island residents add 7% sales tax					$________
Postage and Handling: Add $3.50 for regular shipping and $5.50 for rush shipping.					$________
			TOTAL		$________

Name: ________________________________

Address ________________________________

____

____

Phone: ________________________________

Email: ________________________________

THANK YOU FOR YOUR ORDER!